# HOW TO: GET YOUR WEBSITE NOTICED

**Filip Matous** has a decade of experience bringing eyeballs to websites, and blending knowledge, strategy and execution with case studies and proven methods. With agency experience in Los Angeles, New York and London, Matous has worked with clients including High Speed 1, Marriott International, the City of London Corporation and the *Harvard Business Review*.

You can also find him speaking at conferences and workshops on scaling web traffic and using analytics (including Google Campus, Microsoft and the how to: Academy). In 2012, he was named a marketing 'Young Master' by EntrepreneurCountry magazine.

**how to: ACADEMY** launched in September 2013. Since then it has organized over 400 talks and seminars on Business, Lifestyle, and Science & Technology, which have been attended by 40,000 people. The aim of the series is to anticipate the needs of the reader by providing clarity, precision and know-how in an increasingly complex world.

FILIP MATOUS

# HOW TO: GET YOUR WEBSITE NOTICED

bluebird
books for life

First published 2016 by Bluebird
an imprint of Pan Macmillan
20 New Wharf Road, London N1 9RR
Associated companies throughout the world
www.panmacmillan.com

ISBN 978-1-5098-1449-7

9 8 7 6 5 4 3 2 1

A CIP catalogue record for this book is available from the British Library.

Printed and bound by CPI Group (UK) Ltd, Croydon, CR0 4YY

# Contents

**Part Three: Measurement and Optimization**

# Introduction

*'I'm honestly freaking out, are we going to be okay, Filip? I've got a family and staff to support, if we lose our website traffic our company is screwed.'*

I was freaking out too. Our old boutique agency had taken a low-seven-figure Australian tour client through a whole website evolution including a new brand, layout and structure. And upon launch, the visitor count dropped.

The problem was that the four-person development team I had hired to build the website had blundered – big time. I had made the wrong choice in supplier and could now be responsible for sinking a financially healthy business. The new website wasn't bringing in the traffic source responsible for over 70 per cent of their business: people searching Google for tour providers in their niche. And Google traffic needs a well-built website for rankings and traffic.

Of course, while all this was going on I had to keep mentally tough. I needed to serve our other agency clients, fulfil my responsibilities to my business partner, and when I went home each night, present a human face to my fiancée.

I'll explain how we turned that situation around, but first I need you to understand my aim in writing this book.

This is the kind of stuff that keeps me up at night. When, with all the best will in the world, website strategy goes pear-shaped and good people stress out because either know-how or know-who isn't up to scratch. Basically, I hate making poor decisions and get huge pleasure from knowing that I've made the right moves.

There's a lesson you'll learn throughout these pages, which is contained in what I said above: *a business with only one revenue stream, one source of traffic, one way to get noticed, is too vulnerable.* This book will show you how to get more of your market to visit your website, and thus protect you from a single point of failure.

Elon Musk, the most effective person alive today, compares topical knowledge to a semantic tree. If you have a website with some traffic coming to it but you don't fully understand how it all works, you have a tree without a trunk. You'll keep learning about different branches and leaves, but without the fundamental principles in place there's nothing stable to hang on to.

Allow me to help build your tree trunk.

Are you in? Devote the four hours it will take you to read what I have to say, and I guarantee that when you put this book down you will understand how to scale what is working, remove what isn't, and create results for your business.

As for that tour-business crisis . . .

Once we worked out the root of the problem and captured the flow of traffic from Google, the company saw a 70 per cent increase in sales. The impact was so strong that the business owner temporarily stopped any additional efforts to gain more traffic in order to find a new office and hire more staff to handle the increase in email and phone inquiries.

Suddenly we were all sleeping a lot better. And if you are struggling to get your website noticed, you'll soon be sleeping a lot better too.

# How I Got Started

My interest in driving website attention began when I worked in LA as an intern at an agency looking after the Air Jordan and Sony PlayStation accounts. My boss showed me the legendary seven-minute clip of Alec Baldwin's sales monologue in *Glengarry Glen Ross* (if you haven't seen it, put your coffee down and have a look).

Those seven minutes changed my life.

Little did my boss know that I would build a career on that monologue and put this approach at the centre of what I do.

I moved to NYC to work at an agency on iconic Madison Avenue, diagonally opposite the Flatiron Building. My job was pitching to bloggers games and toys from the agency's Hasbro toy account. Seeing the bloggers write about whatever I had pitched fascinated me. I wanted to know how the attention they brought to each item impacted sales.

Moving to London, I worked for another agency where I pitched to bloggers whatever mobile phone we were selling and learned to measure the traffic behind their blogs. I enjoyed analysing the website and traffic game much more than the process of pitching, so when I had the opportunity to work for the Head of Media at the City of London Corporation to set up their first foray into social media – which bloomed into eighty separate social-media channels – I quit my agency job. It was 2009 and organizations were starting to take web traffic seriously.

Shortly afterwards, together with my friend Sam Kidby, I set up a boutique web-traffic agency. We ran it together for five years, buying and using just about every kind of web traffic that existed. We worked for smaller companies who needed websites to grow their business, larger clients like Marriott and *Harvard Business Review*, and lastly with other marketing agencies wanting to make sense of their traffic.

*How to: Get Your Website Noticed* contains all the lessons I've learned and mistakes I've made after a decade, and about 25,000 hours, of working on my craft. I have drawn on my website experience, the hundreds of technical books I've read, and the wisdom I've garnered from my network of peers. It will make your head hurt a bit, and change your perspective on the symbiotic relationship between your website and those who visit it. It will also, if you take action, help to grow your business.

Let's roll.

# Glossary

Here are the main terms you'll find in this book.

**Ad**: any advertisement that you paid for to get traffic to your website.

**Analytics**: communication of the patterns found in the metrics; logical analysis that is future-focused.

**Autoresponder**: an automated email sequence that starts when someone opts in.

**Backlink**: a link that points to your website from an external website.

**Bounce**: when someone comes to your web page and leaves without visiting a second page. Nothing to do with time on page.

**Click-through rate (CTR)**: the ratio of people who clicked vs those who had the option to click.

**Conversion rate**: the ratio of people who converted to a goal vs those who had the option to do so.

**Cost Per Acquisition (CPA)**: the cost for someone to take whatever step you want them to take.

**Domain**: the url of your website, aka yourname.com.

**Empathy**: the most important concept in this whole book.

**Funnel**: any sequence of traffic with a goal at the end.

**KPIs**: Key performance indicators (usually target metrics).

**Landing page**: the first page a website visitor lands on.

**Market**: The total audience online that is relevant to your website.

**Metrics**: the numbers, presently and in the past.

**Opt in**: to subscribe or give an email in exchange for something.

**Opt out**: to unsubscribe.

**Persona**: your ideal website visitor.

**Traffic**: sources, channels, visitors, people, users – all various ways of explaining the people that land on your website. Traffic can be cold, warm or hot – temperatures that represent how familiar and interested a visitor is in your website.

**UTM**: simple code to attach to a URL to track a traffic source, medium, and campaign name.

## Part One

# HOW YOUR WEBSITE STRATEGY IMPACTS YOUR BUSINESS GOALS

Those of you aged over thirty will remember the primitive websites created in Geocities, and the bleeps and blurps made by a 56K modem trying to connect so that you could surf Netscape. I sure do. I was fifteen and in high school when my teacher pulled my parents into a meeting. 'Your son is the only student in my class still writing homework on a typewriter. He needs a computer.'

I also remember messing about on my mum's computer and somehow getting a virus on the black-and-orange screen. Perhaps it was from the 5.25 inch floppy I was using. All it said was 'Your computer is stoned' and I cried because I thought I had broken it. I didn't know what *stoned* meant.

But keeping up with the evolution of the internet is what I'll be doing for a very long time. I sigh when I hear people say 'Websites are dead!' Some gurus try to argue that all they need is social media to represent their business, but let me assure you: websites are more alive than ever and I know the numbers intimately. Meanwhile, the internet is morphing out of its awkward teenage years and turning into a grown-up.

Now more than ever websites can make or break your business. They are the primary place for people to find you online, to research you, and to decide if they trust you. For example, I see that the About page and team page of all the service-based clients I've worked for gets visited before and after an initial meeting takes place. Product-based businesses know their website is the cheapest and often most important shop front they have.

To prepare for the first chapter, I want you to think about the main ways you find new products or services.

McKinsey calls this *the consumer-decision journey*. It loosely includes:

- **Initial consideration**: mentally shortlisting brands based on brand perceptions and recent touch points (set off by a trigger/need)

- **Active evaluation**: the process of researching potential purchases and adding and subtracting brands as they evaluate what they want

- **Sales moment**: finally selecting and purchasing one brand

- **Post-purchase experience**: the consumer's expectations are tested against reality and inform the next customer journey

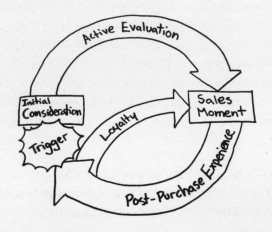

This matches up with some of the ways you find services and products, doesn't it? While I don't discuss loyalty, it's important to see how it all fits together.

Now let me throw in the role played by your website during the *initial consideration*. There are four ways a brand is shortlisted:

1. **Store/agent/dealer interactions** – not something your website can help with

2. **Consumer-driven marketing** – ever-potent word-of-mouth, online research, reviews (your website may play a part in due diligence)

3. **Past experience** – your website may play a part if it's a repeat customer

4. **Company-driven marketing** – your company's efforts to reach the market

The specific type of website you will need is something we'll cover in Chapter 1. But first let's sort out the framework for getting that website noticed. Stick with me, it's important we cover this before heading into Chapter 1.

I'll use my obsession with Alec Baldwin's character in *Glengarry Glen Ross* to illustrate how your website works with *company-driven marketing*. As he's shouting at Jack Lemon's salesman character and pulling his big brass balls out of his laptop, he focuses on the chalkboard where the four letters spell A–I–D–A.

- <u>A</u>TTENTION: The source of traffic
  This is what this book is all about: how you get noticed by your market. Getting traffic.

- **INTEREST**: The first website visit
  Your website content. Where cold traffic goes. This is Part I of the book and it's essential to get right before we worry about getting noticed. Because if the visitors come and you can't keep them interested, you've wasted time building something that doesn't work.

- **DESIRE**: The repeat visits
  This is also in Part I, and is harder than keeping someone interested. Taking someone from being interested to salivating at the mouth takes skill, strategy and the right content. And more often than not, it takes multiple touch points and site visits.

- **ACTION**: The conversion
  If you get desire right, this part follows naturally. Action might mean an email or phone call lead. Or it might mean a sale. Or if you are building your platform or brand it might mean an email subscriber, or a social-media follower.

*'Get them to sign on the line which is dotted.'*

The following four chapters will teach you:

1. What kind of website you need to match your business – and the main pages you should use

2. The role your brand plays in making an effective website – this covers imagery, copy and identity

3. User experience and the traffic funnels you need to map out to make your website's visitors' experience a good one

4. The content you need to attract the right traffic

# 1:

# WEBSITES AND PAGES

## 1.1  Website Types

### What kind of website do I need?

You might already have a website. You might be looking to update an existing one or to build a new one from scratch. Start by asking yourself the following questions (if you aren't looking to build a site or understand the full cycle of costs, skip to the section 1.2 on page types):

### *Am I selling my company or myself, and do I just need a brochure online?*

Perhaps a *static one-page brochure site* is all you need. These can be made without a Content Management System (CMS), which often means it's much harder to update if you aren't a developer, but cheaper to create. And it loads fast online. You can also look at one-page scrolling parallax websites. These are becoming very popular because they look cool and give depth to your website.

### Do I plan to create content for my site on a regular basis?

If the answer is yes, you will want a dynamic content site with a CMS. The gorilla CMS in this space is WordPress. It runs about a fifth of the world's websites. Although it began for blogs, it's grown to run all kinds of websites including ecommerce. Even some large news sites like TechCrunch use WordPress.

### Am I going to sell any products or services directly through my website?

Yes? You are looking for an *ecommerce website*. These often cost a lot because they need to be secure and flexible, and handle payments. Magento and Shopify are the most popular website CMSs who handle this.

### Am I building a community or membership site?

Self-explanatory, but you are either looking to build your own membership site, or you might use one of the existing platforms that serve this function. There are plenty of third-party modifications (called plugins) for WordPress sites that turn them into membership websites. If you run physical events sites, meetup.com might be a fit.

### Am I building a directory?

You might want a directory blended with a content CMS. Drupal, Joomla and WordPress are all popular options.

The majority of websites fit into one of these categories or are a blend. Let's now discuss how much this all costs.

# How much should it all cost?

First let's break apart all the components of a website and then attach costs:

## Domain

This is the website address. Popular providers of this are GoDaddy and 1&1. Expect a typical domain name to cost about £7 to £35 a year. Now pretty much all the short, good URLs have been bought. Expect to spend anywhere from a few thousand to over 30K for a premium short domain that ends in .com, .net or .org. The sky's the limit for those with great-sounding domains, and often the brand makes the investment worth it if your company is earning in the upper-six-figure or higher space.

## Hosting

Pretty much never get the cheap hosting that you can buy from the same company you bought your domain name from. It sucks. Without going into details, any hosting under £7 a month just isn't going to be great. You don't need to be spending hundreds a month if you are a small company, but for reference I spend about £70 a month combined for five small sites and I consider that middle-of-the-road. More expensive solutions include RackSpace and Amazon, and with hosting, what you pay is often indicative of the results.

The cheaper solid providers I have had good experiences with include Site5, SiteGround and WPEngine (the latter is great for those on WordPress).

Whatever you are spending, the important thing is that your website loads up in under a few seconds. Five seconds is the absolute max and that is already far too long, resulting in higher rates of people abandoning the site. I like to hit the two-second mark.

Understand what a Content Delivery Network (CDN) is, as it might be a game changer for your site-speed, especially if you have many images. Popular providers include CloudFlare and Amazon.

### Brand identity

This means all the visual aspects that form your overall brand. It might be found in the website designer, but often logo work needs a specialist. Good logos usually cost £1K and up. Sure, you can get a £70 logo designed but it's going to feel like that. There's a reason good logos cost thousands.

### Website design

I've worked with designers who charge from a few hundred a page to a couple of thousand a page. Having learned what good design does to website results I usually go for the higher-end stuff.

Most people new to design don't realize that for each page designed, about three versions need to be created to match Desktop, Tablet and Mobile views. That's without going into retina display on Apple and other resolution issues.

### Frontend development

This is everything you can see on a website. A frontend developer needs to be able to take a designer's Photoshop files and slice them up and make them work on a real web browser. *Pixel perfect* is something you are looking for here. A frontend designer will have an understanding of HTML, CSS and JavaScript.

### Backend development

All the frontend needs to live somewhere. A backend developer is in charge of the data, the server, the application and the database. It's the stuff visitors don't see but supports the frontend. You need backend to manipulate data.

I like to think of the designer as the interior designer, the frontend as the team who realizes the designer's vision, and the backend as the actual construction of the house.

### Full-stack development

In some cases where the site is a brochure site, you can get away with a full-stack developer, someone that can do both. But just like, say, a baker and a chef, most people are better at one than the other, and a jack-of-all-trades, once the website gets complex, is rarely a good idea.

And yes, I've used a designer that is a full-stack developer and while the results weren't great, they did exactly what was needed. Just expect these to not cost that much and the quality to not be that good.

### Maintenance

It used to be common to have monthly retainers with the web team who hosted your site but I don't recommend this if you are a smaller company or sole owner. It's too easy to pay for the hosting directly and have a contractor who is an email or phone call away should anything go wrong. Things rarely go wrong, however, if the site is built well and if hosting was set up correctly from the start.

Sites like codeable.io are making monthly retainers extinct. This doesn't apply if you are a deeper seven-figure company, as you may already have an IT team in-house.

### And how many years should my website last?

The shelf life of your average website is about three years. Five years is too long – in five years a site shows its age.

What doesn't change is the site architecture (more on that later) and the core pages, if they were built strategically. It's good practice to touch up the design every year or so, after looking at what the rest of the market is doing.

For example, five years ago the majority of websites were not responsive (mobile friendly). Now they must work on mobiles – it's not an option. Even popular social networks change in that time, so if you have a blog with social-media share buttons you may need to swap one network for a newer, more popular choice.

## 1.2   Page Types and Their Purpose

The main work-horses: Homepage, About, Team, Contact, Content/Blog, Offer/Sales Page, Campaign Landing Page.


### Homepage

*In one sentence: Where visitors want to understand the purpose of your company.*

The biggest common mistake I see in homepages is too much stuff being thrown on there. A visitor lands on the page and finds all sorts of calls to action (CTA), requests to click on this, read that, scroll here, check out this social media, etc. Don't do this if you want a good first impression of your website.

Your homepage should answer these questions for the visitor:

- What is the purpose of this website and company?

- Does the brand strike you as trustworthy and interesting enough to devote a few minutes of your time?

- How might investigating this website benefit you?

It's also the page that displays the four prominent parts of your brand:

- Name

- Logo

- Your sales moment[*]

- Hero image

In short, you want to answer the questions that someone in the *initial consideration* phase might have about your own company.

Those who visit your homepage are likely to either know or have heard about you. Traffic is usually traced back to people searching for your brand name on Google, or clicking a link in an email footer, or by word of mouth. It's not the page that most of your traffic will go to if you are actively marketing your website. If you are actively marketing, you'll

---

[*] James Connor's wonderful book *The Perfection of Marketing* goes into brilliant detail on all these parts, especially what a sales moment really is.

want tailor-made landing pages that match the source of traffic.

We'll get to how to find your sales moment, but for the moment think of it this way. It will be the most prominent sentence on the page, near the top and in the biggest font. It has to tap into the reason people would say 'Yeah, this is worth my time.'

Optional: A short explainer video goes a long way to crank up interest for many new visitors, and you should set up the main action you want people to take – such as getting in touch – after visiting the homepage.

Finally, don't forget to make it easy to get in touch. One 50-person company forgot to link to their address at the bottom of the homepage, and once we did link it we found it was used at least once a day.

Essential reading on website pages: Steve Krug's book *Don't Make Me Think* (2005).


## The About page

*In one sentence: Where people go to learn about who you are and how that could benefit them.*

The About page isn't about you. It's about how you can help the visitor. Don't try to be clever, just call it *About*.

This page is great for sharing a short story that connects with the visitor emotionally. Make sure the narrator's name and photo are also on the page. I don't recommend cartoons or other representations. Use your name and a quality image that matches your brand tone. And don't be boring – a common mistake.

The About page leads on to the team or individual bio page(s). Make this navigation easy.

## Team/People page

*In one sentence: Where visitors go to get an understanding of who they spoke with or are going to speak with.*

If you have a team of fifty or fewer employees, I recommend a page that lists everyone together, with individual pages for the staff who are client-facing.

This is so important, because these pages are visited by people either prior to or right after meeting with someone. I see the same three-day timeframe (day before, day of the meeting, day after) of visitors coming to individual bio pages.

After the content pages and the homepage, the team-member pages are the most visited – because humans want to know about the other humans they are dealing with.

## Contact page

*In one sentence: Where people go to get in touch and find your address.*

Keep this simple, list the relevant contact phone number(s) and email(s) and postal address. Don't go overboard with social-media links. It's very common to have an email form on these pages, but from my experience having an email in plain text above the form allows people to choose how the email is sent. The plain-text email will usually get used more than three times the amount the contact form is used.

This is the page that almost never gets visited first in a website session, but is often visited last. It's common to see an exit rate (when people leave your site) of over 90 per cent here if you look at your analytics. This is normal.

## Content/blog post

*In one sentence: Where visitors go to get educated, entertained or both.*

Content pages such as blog posts, videos, and case studies are great pages to send new visitors to. This is because good content pages educate and/or entertain and are usually the best way to warm up cold traffic.

They are replacing the sales page as the most common landing page (the first page new visitors see).

## Offer/sales page

*In one sentence: Where visitors go at the active-evaluation phase or moment of purchase.*

This is a crucial page if you sell products . . . obviously, Sherlock. A huge thing overlooked by most people are the different shopping habits used on a device. Given our rising mobile and tablet use, and growing comfort with completing a purchase on a mobile phone, sales pages need to be designed separately for these devices.

You know when you visit Amazon and don't buy whatever product you were watching, and then see that product show up all over the internet and on your Facebook feed? The sales page is a prime candidate for contextual remarketing, where the product the visitor was looking at is added to a retargeting list that is marked as a purchase completion that didn't occur.

Most professional ecommerce optimizers will run many a/b tests on these pages to get them working as well as possible.

Be mindful that a sales page works way better with warm and hot traffic. This means that the visitor has already investigated your brand and is comfortable shortlisting you right up to the moment of purchase. Conversely, if you send cold traffic (new to you or your brand) it usually causes a very high bounce rate.

### Is my site easy to use?

Step a few feet away (try ten feet) from the screen and ask yourself if it's obvious what the visitor is supposed to do next – and repeat it on every main page of your website. The call to action (CTA) should be visually obvious and not compete with those features that are not the main CTA.

This question requires you to not use your gut, and to earnestly consider if it is straightforward. The one main thing that each page is supposed to do (there are never two main things, if you've prepared properly) should jump out at you.

For one communication agency I advise, we used software called CrazyEgg and it allowed us to see heat maps of where people moved their mouse on their website. After a few thousand visitors on each page we knew what features where being used and what was being ignored. We could also pull apart scroll depth and found many pages that just didn't have good percentages of people who made it all the way down to the bottom of a given page. Combining this with exit rates and conversion rates, we were confident about moving features around, stopping once the heat maps showed that each feature on screen played a role and that all the pages were being used.

Using basic data to eliminate what isn't good on a website is so much easier than trusting your gut. There are many different software solutions, such as ClickTale, that help answer the question 'Is my site easy to use?' by taking screen recordings of people using it. You can then have the most boring popcorn night of your life as you rewatch the recordings. But for an analytical mind it plays like a thriller – you can see nuances that you never thought possible in the ways that people use your site.

Of course you can use eye-tracking and neuroscience by hooking people up to brain-scanning equipment as they go click on your pages, but that gets much more expensive. Agencies like lab.co.uk are making serious progress in website neuroscience.

But there is one final way to get a cheap grip on what people think of your site, and that's by using usertesting. com where, for about £35 per tester, you can list a bunch of questions you want to learn about your site and they record a video of the person using it along with their audio feedback. I've employed this service and found it a very helpful process for getting honest feedback on how easy your site is to use.

## What the hell is information architecture (IA) and why do I need it?

The phrase 'the structural design of shared information environments' probably elicits the same reaction as when someone says 'yes, interest rates are problematic.' You make a serious adult face like you know what the heck they are talking about.

Let me say what IA is in one crude sentence: IA is usually a one-page document that maps out how all the different pages and parts of your website link together so you can make the end result easy to navigate – and not totally suck because it's a poorly thought-out mess.

Blech.

Let me try a bit harder. The main purpose of information architecture is to sort out how everything on your website works together. I prefer a comprehensive flow that shows how all the pages link, plus all the traffic sources at the top, and finally all the software involved.

Here is a super simple diagram of IA:

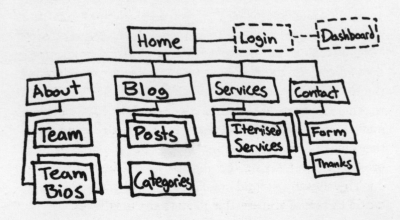

At minimum, IA needs to sort out:

1. **Page Hierarchy** – the layers of pages and how they link to each other.
2. **Navigation** – how users are to move from one page onto the next.
3. **Label Content types** – list all the different types of content that will be on your website.

Lately I've been involved with scaling the amount of attention one podcast gets. Now, no IA ever took place in the beginning because the podcast owner didn't expect it to take off in popularity the way it did. The podcast guests are the cream of the crop, and the attention keeps growing.

But the site is often sluggish or not online when it counts, the traffic from Google is non-existent even though each episode is listened to by at least a couple of thousand people, and the social-media shares are into the multiple hundreds.

Even the way the site links to iTunes and other podcast providers is backwards, and the team is frustrated with the technical limitations. The show is – and of course I'm biased – exceptional. But the existing IA holds it back. So before any revamp takes place I need to map everything out. The result of this one-page IA document means that the new designer and the front- and backend developers can take the existing content and lift it onto a professional tech setup that will last for years.

The beauty of well-done IA is that while your websites may change every three years or so, the basic layout stays the same and allows for growth. Never begin a new website project without taking the time to do IA, because if you don't, eventually a world of pain awaits and you will have to tackle IA before you are able to go to the next level.

# 2:

## BRAND

In 2010, with Marko Saric (of howtomakemyblog.com), I ran the London Blog Club. It was a collection of about 500 London-based bloggers, with skill-levels ranging from amateur to those making a full-time living from blogging. Seeing all these different levels, it was clear that what separated the amateurs from those earning money were two things:

1. Discipline in delivering monthly to weekly quality content.
2. An investment in a considered brand.

At the time I was running two blogs, standstrong.tv, a video blog where I got to interview heroes of mine like Stephen Covey, and enviableworkplace.com, a blog that focused on company culture (which I run with my mate Andy Partridge to this day).

Neither blog had a brand when they began, but learning from the others, I invested in nice designs and spent about £700 on each logo. And sure enough, both times when the redesign went live, the time people spent on the page increased and my repeat traffic went up. But why? Is this correlation or causation?

I've seen over and over that something as intangible as the emotion conveyed by a brand has massive impact on traffic and results. It's the feeling a website visitor is left with after they leave your site. It's what identifies and separates you from others. It's the foundation of a good website and encompasses tone, image and emotion.

Since then I've become interested in understanding the impact of brands and have learned to spot what separates a well-thought-out brand from one that just looks nice. I've learned that you can see the results of good branding hidden in the numbers.

## 2.1 Branding – How Do I Represent Myself and My Company Online (and Offline)?

Here is a two-part exercise to help you understand who you are going to serve your website to.

### How to start a brand or revamp one: the empathy-mapping process

There's a straightforward framework to follow if you want to get close to what shape your brand should take in moving forward. At the end of performing this framework you'll have the right brand name, the right logo, the right sales moment / slogan and the right image to represent your brand.

Not only that, but *empathy mapping* combined with persona creation (next section) will turbo-charge how effective your traffic-generation methods are.

There's no point getting noticed if the brand doesn't match your ideal website visitor.

Empathy mapping takes about one to two months to properly do. I've used it a dozen times with clients and you can't beat the results. It removes the guesswork and leaves you with a brand that matches your market.

Let's for the sake of clarity define empathy and what we are trying to achieve.

**Empathy**: Putting yourself in someone else's shoes. The identification with the feelings, thoughts and attitudes of others – and then experiencing those feelings, thoughts and attitudes yourself. Essentially feeling what they feel, for a brief moment of time.

**What this achieves**: If you can tap the emotions that your market experiences and what they want from a brand, you can shape your product or service to fit their expectations.

**Warning**: Your company brand will involve your values as a business but the visual result isn't about what you like, it's all about what matches your market. I don't care if one or another logo excites you, if one or another slogan excites you, I want the market to validate it. This works best with existing customers, but if you are starting up, find people who are your ideal customer.

- **Step 1**: Identify the best customers that you've had. This might mean their spending habits or the type of people they are. Ask at least ten of them to give you thirty to forty minutes each of their time. If you can ask twenty people, even better.

- **Step 2**: Take them through this framework and ask

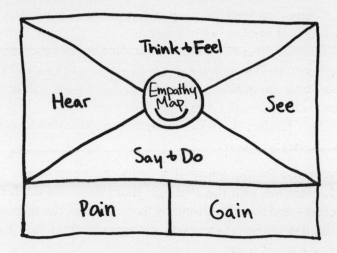

the following questions. You should tailor these to fit the interviewee, but the root of the four sections plus the Pain and Gain stay the same:

**Opening explanation of what the purpose of the call is (5 mins)**

*See (5 mins)*

- Who surrounds you? Who do you spend time with?
- What media do you use?
- What types of offers are you exposed to daily?
- What problems / annoyances do you encounter?

*Think & Feel (5 mins)*

- What's really important to you that you might not say publicly?

- What moves you?
- What are your dreams and aspirations?

### Say & Do (5 mins)

- What do you tell others? What do you brag about?
- What hobbies do you have?

### Hear (5 mins)

- What do your friends say?
- Who really influences you? How?

### Pain (5 mins)

- What keeps you up at night?
- What are the risks you fear taking?
- What are the obstacles between you and your goals?

### Gain (5 mins)

- How do you measure progress and success?
- What are some of your strategies for achieving your goals?
- What gets you going in the morning?
- What are your hopes and dreams?

### Your brand questions (only for those that have used your brand in the past) (5 mins)

- Why did you choose our brand?
- How did you feel before you used our product?
- How do you feel after you use our product?

- Fill in the blank: 'Brand XXXX' is: _____

Once this is completed you should share your findings with the team, if there is one. Group the responses and look for patterns. Next, we'll learn how to turn this into personas – a complementary addition to empathy maps.

### Persona creation

*In one sentence: A persona means a fictional person that represents your ideal website visitor (customer) with their goals, needs and interests, and defined demographics.*

You might have a few. Here's how one persona might look for a company that sells DIY courses on transitioning your hobby to a professional career:

*primary persona: the main user type*

## Dasha DIY:
### Interior Design Hobbyist
*"My best Friday nights are when I stay home and work on projects"*

Early 30s, 1st time home owner

Secondary school teacher dreams of turning DIY hobby into career

**Quick take on Dasha**

Computer skills: Average
Prefered device: iPad
Top sites: Pinterest & Imgur
Avg. weekly DIY: 15 hours
Fav. Netflix: Fixer Uppers

**Key goal(s)**

Dasha wishes she could spend more time DIYing her home.

She would like to learn what it takes to transition her hobby into a part-time career.

**A day in the life**

Dasha is pretty sure her friends think she's a bit weird with the amount of time she spends on DIY projects.

Her fiancé comments that she is rarely found around the home without paint on her clothes.

Dasha's commute is often spent listening to podcasts and audiobooks by streaming her iPhone to her car stereo. Isn't aware of any good DIY podcasts.

Weekends usually involve DIY and visits to Homebase and Squire's Garden Centre.

Now, this exercise can easily cost six figures when run by a consultancy for a larger brand, and of course it carries much more detail than shown above. But in many cases you can do a stripped-down version and get the results you need. And by results I mean how traffic reacts even before it hits the first page of your website. Part II of this book covers the source of the attention.

The battle to get people to stay and take some action on your website is won and lost in this research. I never skip this persona phase on medium or larger projects. For small projects where no budget is available you can use secondary research about your market, and that's better than no persona at all. But it's never going to replace actually talking with your market.

The good news is that after you have conducted an empathy map, you'll have the majority of the data you need to put a persona together (there may be more than one). You'll just need to combine some demographic data, and you're good to go.

Before we learn how to make one, let's explore who uses personas: the marketing and operations departments of your company. Marketing need to know which personas are worth targeting and operations need to know for whom the product or service is being built or optimized.

There might be some nuance in personas:

- **Marketing personas**: demographics, buying preferences, messaging, emotional triggers, media habits.

- **Product/Service design personas**: less emphasis on demographics, more on behaviours, end goals and why people do what they do.

If you look at the questions in the empathy map you'll see a blend of both types, and while you may need to place emphasis on different attributes for marketing and operations I'd just make one blended persona and paint a rounded picture.

In the next section, we'll get into messaging. And that's almost impossible without having done this work.

## 2.2 Copywriting: Tone, Chutzpah, and Fighting Boredom, the #1 Offender

'Copy cannot create desire for a product. It can only take the hopes, dreams, fears and desires *that already exist* in the hearts of millions of people, *and focus those already existing desires onto a particular product.*' – *Eugene Schwartz*

*Breakthrough Advertising* by Eugene Schwartz is better than anything I can hope to write; it's free and in the public domain. Visit filipmatous.com/supplement or just email supplement@filipmatous.com and I'll send you the pdf.

Anyhow, what Eugene said is the main point of these next three sections. You won't win if you aren't realistic about your market's emotions and buying triggers. And realism can only come through knowledge, gained by empathy mapping, persona work and information about the existing competition – something we'll discuss in Chapter 5.

So let's start with one pain-point missed by many people trying to put the right messaging into their USP: ensuring that the top sentence on the page resonates with the visitor.

## Messaging

Following Eugene's logic, we need to create a line that arouses interest in the website visitor: 'Yeah, this sounds like it might be for me, I'm going to investigate.'

This isn't the tagline I'm talking about, which often just adds some emotion to your name. What I'm talking about is the USP, which should be the most obvious line at the top of any landing page.

In most cases, clarity trumps persuasion. Clarity educates and persuasion manipulates. Modern marketing is more about providing utility and entertainment than it is about being crafty.

What I like to do, once all the empathy mapping has taken place, is isolate the most common benefit and pain point that I hear and blend the results into one line.

When Sam Kidby and I started Evergreen Reputation we used the tagline 'For All Seasons'. We realized that it didn't say anything about what the benefits of working with us were. We were trying to be clever. So we spoke with our clients and asked what the main benefits were. Over and over we noticed a pattern and turned their words into: *We drive quality traffic to your website to grow your business.*

Unsexy, eh? And it worked. New clients understood what we were about much faster. The benefit was that we were good at getting traffic to websites and the pain point, and real reason for engaging with us, was to positively impact business, which low-quality traffic was unable to do. It seems obvious, looking back.

There are also a few different formulas that work well in creating a good USP headline; here are five of my go-to formulas:

1. **Hero Formula** = *Core want* of your customer + *pain* associated with the want + how *product* solves it

This formula works well if you are selling a product. The *core want* needs to be in big text and the pain and product in smaller text.

> ***Moz (a popular software for online marketers) example:***
>
> 'Products to Power Your Online Visibility'
>
> 'Online marketing is complicated, Moz software makes it easy'

2. **Curiosity Formula** = Desired benefit + Something they should know but don't

> ***Mixergy (a podcast for digital entrepreneurs) example:***
>
> '*Learn from* PROVEN ENTREPRENEURS.'
>
> 'What do the top startup founders know that you don't?'

The economic psychologist George Loewenstein calls

this the 'information gap'. Humans feel actual pain when confronted with a knowledge gap. This is why you can't resist the 'You'll never guess what happened next . . .' click-bait articles. We all fall for them. Using this with a light touch can really increase emotion.

3. **Instant Clarity Formula** = End result customer wants + specific period of time + address objections*

   *Dominoes example:*

   'Hot fresh pizza delivered to your door in 30 minutes or it's free'

Why it's awesome: it focuses on the end result, not your actual product or service and, in sales 101 fashion, handles the main objection before the visitor has a chance.

4. **Social Proof Formula** = Persona Match + Actual Number + Result

   *Basecamp example:*

   'Last Year alone, Basecamp helped over 285,000 companies finish more than 2,000,000 projects'

Why it's awesome: Robert Cialdini showed in his 1984 marketer's bible, *INFLUENCE: The Psychology of Persuasion*, that people will do things that they see other people do. This effect is multiplied when it fits the persona.

Now combine that ole psychological move with the

---

* Thanks to Dane Maxwell at The Foundation for this cracker.

benefit and make it real by putting numbers to it (odd numbers often work better) and you are cooking.

5. **Question-Based Formula** = Question addressing the most common objection + Implied benefit

   *Salesforce example:*

   'How do you measure up? Benchmark your organization's social with the Social Scorecard'

   *Client example:*

   'Does the business world really need another book on emotional intelligence?'

We heard over and over that people wcrc getting lost in the amount of books on emotional intelligence so we put the objection front and centre, and traffic started to stick.

## How to remove the *suck* from your copy

I swear, the majority of copy out there is terrible (aka boring). Finding good copy is an exception because too many companies don't write in plain, spoken English, or whatever language they are using.

### The Blah, Blah, Blah Test

The first way to find out if your copy sucks is by using the official *blah, blah, blah* test. Put on your most self-aware mindset and read your website copy. Or if you are too emotionally attached to your website, ask someone you trust to give it to you as bluntly as possible. If their feedback is comforting, it's usually not helpful. It's a pacifier.

As you read your copy, does the voice in your head start going into *blah, blah, blah* mode? Or does it actually feel like you wouldn't be embarrassed to say it word for word to your mother? Hint: your mum isn't impressed with terms like like *cutting edge, innovative, premier,* and other self-congratulatory jargon.

If at this moment of honesty you do hear the *blah*s in your head, congratulations. You've already made it further than most companies do.

One of the best conversion copywriters today is a Joanna Wiebe of Copy Hackers. A conversion copywriter is someone who's paid to make copy that causes people to take whatever action is the goal. She's got this awesome approach to copy that you can use. It's called *So what, prove it.*

### Using 'So what, prove it'

When writing copy for your website, first ask *so what?* If you are writing stuff that doesn't matter much for the visitor, why is it there?

Then if you pass that part, ask *prove it.* Does your website then prove and back up what you are claiming? Are there testimonials that confirm these things? Have you shown that, in fact, you do know what you are talking about?

It's closely related to what my old university Communications professor kept banging on about until it finally stuck in my head: *Show don't tell.* Telling is the same as if someone starts off a joke by telling you, 'Oh I've got this super-funny joke, man . . .' It rarely is.

### What to avoid

I've explained this to clients many times: every time someone comes to your website to read something, you are making a transaction with them even though no money trades hands. Every touch-point counts.

You might ask them for five minutes of their time, and they will give it to you if they feel that the value they get in return justifies the spend. One of my mates who runs a podcast and a blog in the USA says he feels comfortable with a 10:1 ratio. He says that if he misses the mark once in ten times with his articles then his regular readers will stay loyal to him. But once that ratio allows too many weak articles, loyalty disappears because people feel they wasted their time, and if that happens you'll see a very low repeat-visitor percentage on your website.

Boredom is a very naughty word.

Use chutzpah. If your copy is trying to appeal to everyone then it's not built for the personas you identified. This might mean that your tone is humorous, or casual to the point of using curse words, or it's ballsy, or formal. You *do* you, don't ever be generic, inject your voice and tone – and aim for consistency. If your website copy feels so safe that you think it wouldn't alienate anyone, it's boring. And boring copy is the number-one sin you can commit when chasing conversions on a website.

#### Here's a short list of what I avoid:

- Superlatives and intensifiers: 'really', 'very', 'actually', '-ly/-iest' . . . yawn. Without mercy, delete these nap-inducers, they slow down reading speed.

- 'Best', 'premier', 'leading' (have someone external say this about you, never say it about yourself)

- Overused words meant to hype (some of my favourites): 'revolutionary' – yeah, right; 'cutting-edge', or even more gag-worthy, 'bleeding-edge'. Blech. You mean you are trying to stay current by using a word that millions of sloppy websites use to describe themselves? 'Passionate' – just Google 'Our company is passionate about' and watch your eyes dry out; 'innovative' – prove it.

### What good copy often uses:

- Clarity over persuasion or cleverness
- Leads with benefits and supports the benefits with features
- Sounds natural when you read it out loud
- Identifies who it is for and importantly, who it isn't for

### Do I really need a copywriter to get it right?

Some sales copywriters can charge upwards of £20,000 per page. When I first heard what they charged I was blown away. I mean, who the hell would pay that for one page?! But then on reflection I asked myself this:

If I had £100,000 to send traffic to a landing page with one conversion goal, and let's say each visitor cost £1 to bring, and my conversion rate was 3 per cent, what would I pay to get the kind of copy that was able to double this conversion rate to 6 per cent?

Simple maths time:

£100,000 × .03 = 3,000 conversions
(without a copywriter)

*(Total budget – cost of copywriter)*
*× conversion rate = outcomes*

I could in theory pay up to £50,000 of the total £100,000 to a copywriter if I felt they would at a minimum double my conversions. I'd still get 3,000 goals. But what if the conversion rate was better? And let's say the copywriter actually only cost £1,000. That works out to almost double the conversions: £99,000 × .06 – 5,940.

I've learned that effective copywriters can double conversion rates, and often go higher than that. Good copywriters are conversion focused and it's a blend of skilful art and science, and years of measuring the results of their copy.

This is why professional sales copywriting started in direct marketing – an industry where people were paid to keep testing copy to find the right thing to write, to cause a sales-moment trigger to go off in the highest percentage possible of their target market. They did not fall in love with their copy as that amount of ego would stop them from improving; rather they kept changing and testing until they were unable to improve the conversion rate.

So no, you don't always need a copywriter but you do need to be ruthlessly honest about where you are and how good your copy is. Write with *So what?* and *Prove it!* hanging over you and you'll already be ahead of most of the boring copy cluttering the internet.

## 2.3 Pulling It All Together

### Circumstantial relevance

In 2013, I spent an afternoon in NYC learning from Brian Fetherstonhaugh, the Global CEO of Ogilvy One, about how Ogilvy approaches advertising campaigns like Dove's Real Beauty. I learned some high-level approaches to the role of emotions in advertising. But the key lesson came a few months afterwards. The man who brought this meeting together, Todd Herman (toddherman.me), was voted by Ogilvy as the world's greatest salesman. He taught me a concept that I began to apply online and it became my most important professional mind-shift of the year. He explained that Ogilvy and other advertising greats often selected and discarded visual ideas by starting with this concept.

*Circumstantial relevance*. It's what happens in your brain when judging whether or not something is real or fabricated. It's why websites that use stock images instead of authentic photos often plummet in effectiveness (if you've seen a cheesy phone-operator photo on a website you know what I'm talking about).

### Take off your suit, man

A handful of marketers were chatting in a forum discussion. Feedback was requested from a physical trainer and online personality who had commissioned a bunch of photos of himself in a suit with his shirt off. We were all arguing about which photo looked better and Todd jumped in. He explained we were all unequivocally wrong. None of the photos were appropriate.

If it doesn't look like it would happen in real life, visitors experience *cognitive dissonance* (uncomfortable tension that results from holding two conflicting thoughts in the mind at the same time – see George Orwell's *1984*), and that's not good for your business. In the trainer's case, no one naturally poses wearing suit pants and no dress shirt.

Asked what the goal of the photos was, the trainer said he wanted photos on his website that showed off to people who had money that he was strong, healthy and attractive, and that they could be like him.

So what's a contextual situation that shows off your body? What about throwing your young kids in the air on a nice vacation? Or shirtless, covered in mud in a Tough Mudder race? The goal is to take photos of situations that are real. No one embarks on a body transformation to be in a forced photo.

## Campaigns of the Century and men in grey suits shaking hands

This is why Dove's Real Beauty went viral on social media, increased sales and won AdAge's Top 3 Campaigns of the Century. The strategy was 'to make women feel comfortable in the skin they are in, to create a world where beauty is a source of confidence and not anxiety'. Because perfect people in commercials often don't resonate with the market. Bring in real people, with imperfections, and watch your brand's sentiment positivity soar.

One more thing. Greg Williams, an expert in content,

taught me an important lesson when he was head of media at the City of London Corporation. He explained that the absolute worst shot for newspapers is a picture of two men in grey suits shaking hands. Editors at national publications rarely include these images, especially if given a choice between that and a candid photo of the same two men talking where you can see emotion on their faces.

Any time you're in doubt, show what's real and remove the fabrication.

Recommended reading: *Webs of Influence* by Nathalie Nahai (the Web Psychologist) gives a breakdown of the psychology and motivations at play when people visit your website.

## Do I really need to spend money on a logo?

The logo is only an element of your brand identity but it does signal quality. I've had plenty of long discussions and disagreements on the importance of a logo and it does vary by industry but here's where I've come to. I've experienced the positive difference a logo makes when it's the only thing that's changed.

What does a logo need to do?

- Work in black and white

- Reflect your brand personality

- Be easy to identify and read at a glance

- Look trustworthy and fit your industry

- Work at various sizes, as well as looking good in a

square, because so many social networks use square profile boxes

So what should a logo cost, eh? I've found that overall the cost of a logo follows quality. I personally wouldn't spend under 1K on a logo for a business. I've tried 99-dollar logos and they all looked beta. Which is fine, but if you want to come across as established, you probably don't want to look like a hundred bucks.

Also, I don't recommend doing logo work on its own. It should be done in conjunction with identity work and, if you are in a startup, after the business idea is polished, your USP is done and your personas are clear.

# 3:

# TRAFFIC FUNNELS AND STRATEGY

My all time favourite *falsely* attributed quote on the internet claims that Abraham Lincoln said: 'Give me six hours to chop down a tree, and I will spend four hours sharpening the axe.'

This is the approach I want you to take with this chapter. We're going to learn about traffic funnels and I promise the magic is found in not shortcutting the preparation. Then in the following chapter we'll take what's here and learn what content needs to be in the funnel. At this point we'll graduate to Part II of this book and learn to swing the axe.

## 3.1   A Short History of Sales Funnels

### Classic funnels

Back in the early '00s the basic online sales funnel looked like this:

$$Ad \rightarrow Sales\ page \rightarrow Checkout$$

£1 worth of ad traffic was sent to a website sales page and £2 fell from the bottom of the funnel.

Even in 2010 and 2011, I was using this three-step funnel to do lead-generation to sell property. For example:

*Ad → Sales Page → Lead Capture*

**Ads**: Google AdWords, Facebook Ad.

**Sales Page**: Homepage with email capture in the header.

**Lead Capture**: They gave us their email and phone in exchange for a PDF property brochure sent to their email; then the sales team took over to lead nurture.

We managed the client's AdWords account, which had spent over £150,000 directing traffic to a homepage that sold various luxury villas at the 1 to 2 million mark. So the amount we could spend per lead was high. We also added Facebook into the ad mix because of its excellent audience targeting – it too began to provide qualified leads.

Looking back, I have to laugh that we were using the homepage as the landing page. It could have been much more contextual and more effective if we had sent them to tailored landing pages, but it did work at the time.

Early internet riches were won with this simple funnel. But as the number of marketers increased and people become more internet savvy, the funnel started to resemble £1 worth of ad traffic at the top with £1 coming out the bottom in sales. It no longer offered the attractive and easily attainable profit margin of the past.

This forced marketers to innovate. Traffic sources diversified and people tried to find various ways to increase the volume at the top of the funnel. This lasted a few more years. But again, the number of marketers increased and so did the savvy of the average internet user.

That funnel rarely provides a good profit margin any more.

## Modern funnels

So marketers started adding elements to this basic funnel, measuring each step.

This became a popular funnel:

*Traffic Source* → *Content* → *Sales Page*

**Traffic Source**: More content-marketing-based ads, less direct-sales messaging.

**Content**: Educational with sales lightly mixed in. Usually the goal was to get the click from the content page to the sales page.

**Sales Page**: Moves the narrative from educational to buyer intent.

This worked because potential customers liked the soft sell instead of a direct attempt to close a sale or lead.

Let's fast-forward. Now what I've found, along with dozens of other marketers in my network, is that this might be the best overall funnel that exists in 2016:

*Traffic Source* → *Content* → *Retargeting* →
*Contextual Conversion Page*

**Traffic Source**: In this case I'm talking about social-media promoted ads and native advertising (detailed in Part II of this book).

**Content**: <u>Zero</u> sales elements, just educational content.

**Retargeting**: Twitter retargeting, Facebook retargeting, and Google Display and YouTube retargeting.

**Contextual Conversion Page**: a classic sales page with a twist, CONTEXT. The copy references the education acquired from the content page so the visitor feels no disconnect.

## Some other funnels that are hot

Justin Brooke of IMScalable.com is the media buyer to follow if you want to understand the progression of the funnel and where to acquire traffic. Here's a funnel he used in 2015 that could work for mass-market products (the health, wealth and love niches): filipmatous.com/justin-brooke

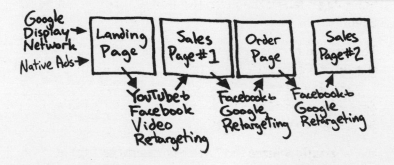

Now I'll add one last funnel that I'm playing with, which might look hard to do but I believe we'll see it more and more. Most of the times I try it I'm seeing positive results. It involves solid PR placements, which makes it more challenging:

## Traffic Source → PR piece → Content → Retargeting**→ Conversion Page

**Traffic Source**: Native and social advertising – this will multiply the amount of people that see the PR placement.

**PR piece**: An educational article that has little to no sales in it but includes a link to the client's website. The PR placement can be an article, podcast, or video – and it needs to appear on a publication that is immediately recognizable and trustworthy for your ideal persona.

**Content**: Either the client's homepage, or preferably, a piece of content such as an in-depth report, whitepaper, video, etc that is relevant to the conversation from the PR piece. The more relevant and tailored, the better this works.

**Retargeting**: The ** comes into play because I sometimes like to extend the amount of non-salesy content someone is exposed to two or three times *and then* use those pages to introduce a conversion page (more sales-focused).

**Conversion Page**: At this point when people come here they've been consuming multiple pieces of content and the trust level should be high. The PR piece being on a trusted publication makes *all the difference* because the visitor transfers their trust of the publication onto your brand.

Note: this funnel probably sounds exhausting, which is the point. You hope that your competition would never bother with a funnel like this. But because it is so long and strategic, it builds trust and is working in ways that I never thought would happen when comparing it to the classic sales funnel. And I think these harder funnels are exactly what keep businesses competitive – those that ignore the evolution will be left behind.

Just read up on Dan Pink's book, *To Sell is Human*. *Non-selling selling* (persuading, influencing, and convincing others in ways that don't involve anyone making a purchase), it's beautiful how this can work online.

## 3.2   Cold, Warm and Hot Traffic

Don't skip this section if you can't explain the difference in traffic temperature. Just as the source of traffic is crucial for matching to your persona, the temperature of your traffic needs to match your content and its order.

Simply:

- Cold: first-time visitor, new to your brand.
- Warm: might be a first-time visitor who heard or read something about your brand, or visited your website a few times and is somewhat familiar with your brand.
- Hot: They know and trust your brand, have probably been on your site more than a dozen times, and are very likely to buy something if you have a product or service that fits their need.

How to treat these temperatures:

- Cold: Unless what you sell is an impulse buy, under £100, try to expose your brand to them in an entertaining or educational fashion. DON'T SELL, BUILD TRUST. Now, the exception is if you have other brands involved that your visitor trusts, for example an event with speakers that are well known to your persona.

- Warm: Keep building their trust. Remember that in most cases, people need many touch-points before they are ready to buy. Your most important role at this temperature is ensuring that every touch-point feels valuable to the visitor and that they want to keep returning.

- Hot: At this point each interaction with your brand has been valuable, and you are ready to introduce your offer. This temperature is most often connected with time. It may take days, weeks or months of touch-points to get here.

Cold traffic is the cheapest, as you may have guessed, and hot traffic is easily a heap more expensive. If you've ever experimented with email marketing you'll know what I'm talking about. When someone says they have a huge list, I don't care; I want to know how many people are warm and hot.

Remember, most times, *not even 4 per cent of your first-time website visitors will buy anything*, no matter the price point. Find reasons to increase repeat visits. Let's learn how.

### How do I warm up a first-time visitor?

Taking what we know about traffic temperature, let's apply it to AIDA – and use the example of trying to get leads to sell consulting services:

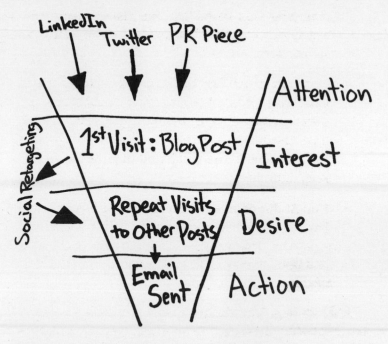

**Attention:** Cold traffic from social media like Twitter and LinkedIn and lukewarm traffic from a PR piece click on a link to come to a landing page on your website.

**Interest:** First-time visitor comes from the source of attention and perhaps reads a blog post, watches a video, and either warms up or dies at this stage. This step must be a good trade of time for value in the visitor's mind or you don't get another chance.

**Desire:** You use retargeting and bring return visits in a short frame of time. Congratulations, you have warmed them up and they may get in touch. Or in a few more visits.

**Action:** Your visitor is ready to have a conversation, so they email you.

It's a heavy-handed analogy, but it's like a romantic relationship. Rush the steps and you get nowhere. Foreplay matters. There is a process and it takes time, but if you are after quality results, you need the courting process.

So back to answering the question. How you get warmer traffic is by assisting your visitor and giving them the space to reach that point themselves. If the traffic is quality (i.e. matches your buyer persona) and they are interested in spending time with your site, you need to respect this and provide the content that helps them to trust and engage with you.

What do I mean by engagement? It might mean:

- Consumption of a blog post: They spent three minutes on your blog post and scrolled to the bottom.

- Lead Magnet: After digesting your content they gave you their email in exchange for a whitepaper, a case study, an educational video that isn't available publicly, an eBook, or even a paperback where they pay for shipping.

- Webinar: They signed up to learn more.

What doesn't work well in most industries is going for the close too fast. Having good content in between the first website visit and the eventual offer is often *the shortest* and most cost-effective route to selling or filling up your lead pipeline.

## 3.3 Funnels – Building the Right Sequence of Pages

Every page should have one job, and it should be obvious. What I recommend at the planning stage of a campaign is to assign traffic sources and pages to each step in the funnel.

### First find out, is your site easy to navigate?

**Accounting-company example**: Last year we helped a company of a dozen or so accountants answer the question of site-navigation ease. By applying CrazyEgg software, looking through the top pages visited and tracking the traffic flow in Google Analytics, it became obvious which pages were resonating and which pages people found boring. These pages were blocking the desired outcome – traffic-temperature increase, which when fixed would result in more leads.

But by looking at time-on-page scrolling patterns in CrazyEgg and the main exit pages in Google Analytics we were able to identify what was working.

Now let's pretend you are in a potential customer's shoes and you want to increase leads through your traffic. Write out each step your target visitor needs to go through.

### UX and UI: understand these terms to communicate what you want to a designer

In one sentence: User Experience (UX) is how people feel going through your website and User Interface (UI) is how they actually interact with your website.

These terms are often fuzzy and can mean different things to different people but they need to work together. I hear these terms used interchangeably rather often, but they are distinct.

To help explain this I asked my mate, the best web designer I know (I'm obviously utterly biased but his work is incredible).

Fast introduction: Marius Ciuchete Paun is a web designer based in Vancouver, Canada, whose desktop and mobile designs have been used by tens of millions of people.

Opposite is our conversation on Slack that sums up the difference between UX and UI and the stages a web page goes through during design.

**Filip:** Is this a web page 'layout'?

**Marius:** Yes. A layout defines the visual structure for an interface.

Also known as a wireframe. It's part of the UX design and it's actually one of the first steps a UX designer needs to go through: identify if it's a one- or two-column website, big photo on the top, etc.

**Filip:** Is this what you would call a 'mockup'?

**Marius:** Yes. Technically, what we have now is called UED (User Experience Design). You know it as UX design. Designers call it 'mockup'.

UX design is the representation of each page – without graphics – with detailed documentation about links and integrations. Think of it as analogous to a blueprint for a building. Page layout of all elements is precise and multilayer actions are

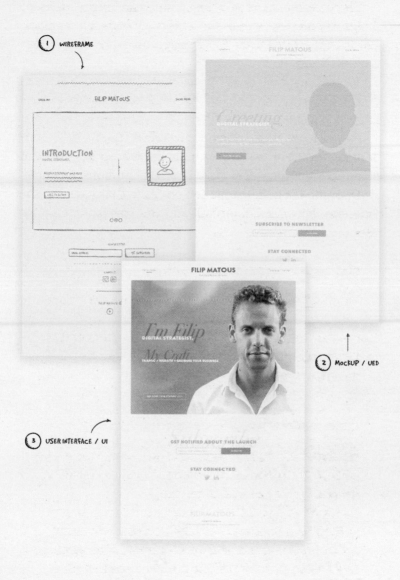

1 WIREFRAME

2 MOCKUP / UED

3 USER INTERFACE / UI

identified, such as pop-ups, links, expanding menus, and other page actions.

UX design is a process, which involves research, interviews, creating user personas, examining the usability and accessibility concerns, and so many other things.

UX design is where you make sure the brand communicates correctly with the consumer, where business goals are defined and where the business strategies are implemented via design patterns.

Notice I haven't said anything about colours, fonts, photos, icons, illustrations, etc? That's because all these fall into –

UID: User Interface Design: The 'candy' area. The part where all designers copy other designers and call it 'inspiration'. LOL.

User interface (UI) is just that: the interface itself. It's the layout, the fonts, the buttons, illustrations, icons, photos, gradients, shadows – anything and everything visual. It's the part of the website that the user actually sees and clicks on.

The reason why UI design is so time consuming is because of the real data involvement.

UX design doesn't require EXACT dimensions, EXACT typography hierarchy (H1, H2, p, div), photo manipulation, EXACT padding to the layout, EXACT grid, EXACT this, EXACT that. It's all based on forms of grey, placeholders, random type, etc.

UI design requires ALL that, and then some more (looking at mobile devices here).

**Filip:** Labour wise, how much effort on the

designer's end (talking per cent) goes into UX vs UI design? 50/50? 70/30? 30/70?

**Marius:** In most cases, UX design is about 35 to 45 per cent of the workload. Sometimes it's 60 per cent, but that's rare (mostly when you build ecommerce websites).

## When has enough testing taken place?

Even before people visit one of your website's landing pages, testing should be taking place at the attention level. The most common is an A/B test – this means testing two variables against each other to find the better one.

For example: you could A/B test your newsletter's email subject's impact on email open-rate by trying two different subjects.

How do you know when you've tested enough? There is the statistically significant answer and the practical answer. I'll confess I rarely follow an academic process.

Something is an improvement after *both* of these points are met on each variable:

- Sample size reaches over 1,000

- Over 100 clicks occur

You can use this process to improve ads, email open-rates, you name it. If it's to make a big impact on business value I'll use one of the calculators online and set a 95 per cent confidence interval. If you are a statistician, you can send hate mail to filipmatous.com/contact.

But A/B testing is applicable for every level from attention to action. Each level has its own challenges and places to improve. There are no perfect funnels.

### Multivariate testing

Testing more than two variations at once. This is the other testing option you have. You'll need a larger sample size for this to work.

You could, for example, test multiple variations on an email list of say 10,000 people.

One way I've used multivariate testing is when picking the right headline for a blog post. As long as I'm targeting quality traffic I'll wait to see how long it takes for each headline to get 100 clicks. The headline that uses the smallest sample size to achieve 100 clicks is the winner. I got this idea when I learned that very high traffic media sites often test the headline live when they hit publish, and after an hour they settle on the winner – i.e. the headline that gets the most clicks.

It's important to stress however that what we are doing is finding a winner based on the click-through rate (CTR). This isn't always the best metric for sales as sometimes the winning variable may filter out the quality traffic by being sensational and attracting the wrong clicks, and the loser, while attracting fewer clicks, attracts the right kind.

You can also have a read on Hubspot, as they have a good introduction to statistical significance: fm.com/statistical-significance.

Oh, one more thing to end this chapter on funnels and strategy.

What do I think savvy marketers will be using as a sales funnel for higher-cost offers in the near future?

*Traffic Source → Content → Retargeting → Follow up content → Retargeting → Follow up content → Retargeting → Follow up content . . .*

No sales page ever.

You might be thinking, 'I should shut this book – Filip is mad.' It's possible that I'm wrong but I doubt it. I think marketing's primary job is to build trust and place your brand in your persona's mind at the time of purchase. This means lots of valuable touch-points. The way the customer journey is evolving, letting the visitor seek out your offers on their own time might be the savviest move you can make.

# 4:

## CREATING CONTENT

### Modern website marketing: education and entertainment

Some of the stuff online marketers talk about makes me want to punch kittens right in the face – I've grown allergic to popular marketing exaggerations. One term that I've heard popularized far too much is 10×. It's often used to show that if you take guru X's advice you'll gain 10× the results. In fitness you do this diet and exercise and blamm-ooh, 10× the results. Just look at how sexy you've become.

Or content marketers saying your content needs to be 10× as good as it was. Isn't, for example, 2× sexy enough? Oh well, I was never good at hype.

What I do agree with is the sentiment behind it. Every year I see the content-quality bar rise. Content that would be shared like mad in 2012 looks average at best in 2016. It's a result of brands noticing that content is a great way to get attention – and sell stuff. I wouldn't say content is getting exponentially better but I feel comfortable saying it doubles in awesomeness every five years or so.

As the big brands shift their marketing budget from traditional channels into online channels, the amount of incredible content rises faster than the supply of people using the internet. It's getting harder for small brands and startups to have any slice of their persona's attention-pie now that the Nike-level brands of the world are spending unreal sums of money creating rad content that directly competes for the attention that the small guys want from their market.

One detail Forrester (a leading market research company) predicts: by the time this book is published, it's very likely that US traditional advertising budgets will be smaller than digital-ad spend.

Smaller niches might be safe from big brands because they are trying to get noticed by smaller fish, but then even the competition and content quality is rising from their similar sized competitors.

## Communications-agency competition

Every year I oversee the update of a competitor report that grades a client against about twenty other London-based agencies competing for the same clientele. These are agencies that poach talent from one another and are often in the same pitches and awards ceremonies. Doing this over the last few years, there are a few things I've noticed when comparing with historic data:

- About every three years, these agencies get new websites

- Video is becoming an important competitive element

- The agencies that put out weak content often shrink in size (not sure about correlation vs causation)

- The humans in the growing agencies seem to have more personal profile on the websites

- Social-media platforms per agency have *decreased*, while usage of the platforms they keep has *increased* (probably a sign of measurement and accountability taking place)

- The third-party measurement and ad-tech software probably doubled in presence on the websites over the last two years

- Email-newsletter frequency has become consistent and so has the format. This isn't too surprising though, as this maturation of digital is happening in every sector and while the internet was a bit of a Wild West, it's growing up.

## 4.1 Why Do So Many People Overestimate How Good Their Content Is?

The first time you start to measure how your content is performing it usually ends in a tearful phone call with your mother: 'But I did my best.'

My expectations on typical content performance are unfortunately close to basement level because I see the numbers every day; most months I have to break the news to people who 'did their best'. The Pareto Principle is alive and well with 20 per cent of the web's content easily taking over 80 per cent of the attention.

If you have no idea how your content is doing visit buzzsumo.com and pop your website URL in and hit enter. Have a look at the amount of:

- Social shares: this gives you an idea of which content is being shared.

- Backlink count: this gives you an idea if any other websites are linking back to your content, which shows authority.

This is just a start, as you should also check stuff like your analytics and see which pages are most popular and how much time is being spent on them. But this is a place to get you started in under five minutes.

There's no escaping the fact that it sucks to find out that the content you've spent time on just isn't helping your business. Or isn't helping it enough to justify the time spent.

This feeling of overconfidence comes from *illusory superiority* (cognitive bias: individuals overestimate their own abilities relative to others) and it's found in and out of work. In a classic example, the University of Nebraska found that '90 per cent of faculty members rated themselves as above-average teachers, and two-thirds rate themselves among the top quarter.'

The hard truth is that without measurement I've found that almost every client overestimates their content, believing it is doing better than the metrics show – and once the data is there, egos are ruffled. Perhaps it's the survival mechanism that we succumb to, trying to make our job or brand sound more valuable than it really is.

But there is something thrilling about measuring your content. It means you can improve, learn from your missteps, and celebrate when content actually works.

We'll learn how to measure and understand the role of metrics and analytics in Part III. Now, let's get some more important web-marketing theory out of the way so we are fully prepared to jump into traffic-generating tactics.


## 4.2  The Modern Role of Marketing: Education and Entertainment


The industry often separates marketing into two camps: outbound and inbound.

**Outbound marketing**: PUSH. It's a megaphone, it interrupts your market and forces its way to their attention. Old-school. Online this looks like email blasts, pop-ups, contextual ads, social-media advertising, banner ads and video ads.

**Inbound marketing**: PULL. It's like a magnet, it aims to interest your market. It's more new-school and it also involves listening and communicating. Online this includes SEO, PPC, newsletters, PR, blogging, organic and some paid social media, content creation, video content and eBooks.

Now, I like both forms of marketing online, and often the two mix well together. There is a school of thought out there that only believes in inbound. For me the potency comes from mixing the two. Create a piece of content that appeals to your target persona, then use inbound and outbound methods to draw attention to it.

## Marketing's modern role

But the big fundamental shift comes back to the start of this book and what McKinsey's customer journey mapped out so well. They say that the main goal of marketing is to *reach customers at moments that most influence their decisions*.

Pre- and post-internet marketing changes this journey in a huge way. Education and the ability to fact check completely destroys the old-school method of buying enough attention and telling people to trust you – even ignoring the word-of-mouth that comes from loyalty. Now, your best bet is to assist them on their journey and provide education as they near their purchase moment. This is why saying you are good/cutting-edge/leading/blah-blah-blah is neutral or harmful to conversions. You need your market to validate you on your website (through testimonials, social proof, and appeals to authority) and off your website through reviews and public relations.

Unless you have a cheap impulse-buy that needs little validation, expect your market – even if they have already bought from you – to audit and judge you against your competitors. And to be put off by your back slaps.

Customer loyalty exists, but it's not as it used to be because of the ability to gather information and the competing free education. The worst (or best!) part is that most marketing-innovation cycles now occur within a window of less than six months.

If something is working on your website, don't be surprised to see your competition have the very same thing in under a year. There might well be people like me pulling apart your marketing funnel for your competition's business intelligence.

## Entertain me

Gary Vaynerchuk says it best: 'Every company is a media company.'

This is massively undervalued in stiffer niches. Yet if you and your competition are both providing great educational content, making it entertaining is the next competitive step. It's why companies like Epipheo can charge five figures for a minute and a half of cartoon video explaining a brand, because they know the sales power of a good story delivered in an entertaining way.

It's why Moz have a weekly online marketing video show and throw jokes and fun outfits into the mix. They know that their market (people like me) are looking to stay on top of online inbound trends, and due to the volume of good resources competing for our attention the entertaining ones get the choice over the dry educational ones. I figure if I'm going to be spending time learning, and if a publisher can make me laugh and occupy my attention span, my reward mechanism will keep me coming back to the content that offers both.

It's why I started putting magic tricks into my *Marketing Not Magic* online video series – I know I'm providing free website marketing education but I want the viewer to enjoy their time on my content so that they come back. And a small percentage of my viewers turn into my customers.

So let me show you how to be so good with your content quality that the competition can't compete.

## 4.3   How to Pick the Right Kind of Content

If your marketing-research budget isn't an issue, I'd say go for a Sysomos MAP account and have them train someone on your team to uncover what kind of content you should be creating by uncovering the top-performing content of your competition. But there is a free and cheap way to get there too.

Here's a process to figure out what kind of content you should be creating. Of course you'll need your personas figured out first, so revisit Chapter 2 if that hasn't been done. It's essential for this to work.

### Pick a journey moment and create your content for that

At what point is your market persona going to need content from you? You need to create content for your persona *at* the stage where they already are.

The numbers may vary but of the *total relevant market* means the amount of people who match your personas, and demographics that could turn into a buyer.

Your relevant market size will be something along these percentages:

- 3 per cent: (A)
  **actively** looking for what you offer

- 7 per cent: (B)
  **passively** looking for what you offer

- 30 per cent: (C)
  **aware** that they need what you offer

- 30 per cent: (D)
  **unaware** that they need what you offer

- 30 per cent: (E)
  **not open** to considering what you offer

### Content for the 3 per cent: (A)
### Actively looking for what you offer

Put your boxing gloves on, read *The Art of War* and proceed. This group is competitive.

These people are close to pulling a trigger on a purchase, have a shortlist, and are most likely spending time on Google researching where to spend their money and tapping their network for advice. The content you create for this group should be salesy, offer plenty of testimonials, and compare your offer to the competition.

You don't need to make content that educates them about their issues because they've already gone through that part of their research. But if you can make your salesy content entertaining, it helps make it stand out from the competition.

Also it's important to note that your competition is probably blowing most of their budget on these 3 per cent because these people are obviously ready to buy. I often like to ignore this group and push the marketing budget into the next three sections as it goes further. I mean, guess where all those expensive Google AdWords clicks are coming from? This minority of your total market is ready to buy.

### Content for the 7 per cent: (B)
### Passively looking for what you offer

These people have a problem to solve or a need to fulfil. They are just about to start, or have already begun, researching where they should spend their money.

Educational blog posts, whitepapers and videos explaining what they should be considering are great at this stage. You can have a touch of sales in this content but try to help them get closer to finding a solution.

### Content for the 30 per cent: (C)
### Aware that they need what you offer

I love marketing to this group because I can get in multiple touch-points before their moment of purchase and, once they trigger into purchase mode, that top-of-mind awareness gives me an advantage over the competition.

No sales tone is needed at this point. The modern funnels we explored in Chapter 3 thrive here. Collateral such as eBooks and whitepapers, accessible by trading their contact email and maybe phone number, is great here.

Blog posts are also the shiznit at this point. You've got time before the purchase so get your brand personality into their head and let it marinate. Also trying to get people on your newsletter's mailing list makes a lot of sense. The best part is even if they never buy, if you offer real value with your content, they may pass on the information to their network via social media, word of mouth and *dark social* (the latter is explained in Chapter 10).

This content is underused because it's unattractive to brands in the following ways. This is because it:

- takes time to convert to a buyer or lead

- is harder/impossible to attribute original touch-point and first-website visit when tracing the final purchase touch-point to the start

- takes a high-level understanding of your market's emotions

And I love it. This is where long-term ROI comes in and it takes patience. Done right, it will build your brand platform, increase your website SEO and leave you with evergreen content that keeps bringing traffic to your website.

If you have a financially stable and growing company, invest into this level and watch what happens a year later. Not all companies have the luxury of such a drawn-out funnel and many companies won't even try to reach this group. That's an opportunity for you, if you are in a position to play the long game.

This kind of content has to emotionally connect with your personas in a place where they are.

### Making it real

**Your offer:** Let's say you are selling software that measures company culture . . . to someone who doesn't quite understand what company culture is, or know that they can even measure it. They are unaware.

**Your buyer**: Let's pretend your ideal buyer is a business owner trying to go from a fifty-person company to a 100-plus company.

What might they be interested in reading, listening to or watching? After your work with empathy mapping, you've learned that they will likely be reading and attending conferences that explain how to scale up business. They might be reading books on business systems, how to build a strong management layer, looking at recruitment issues, office-size issues.

**The content**: So if you create content that talks about an often overlooked 'glue' to hold management, recruitment and business systems together during a time of growth, they might want to know what this glue is. And then when they reach your content they find it is well researched and speaks rationally to their sceptical mind.

And no discussion of buying your software is introduced. Far more foreplay is needed. Instead you offer them a lead magnet, an eBook to learn more about understanding the glue, perhaps some academic studies on culture are included. Or maybe you clearly explain that your newsletter will, once a month, send them all the research you are doing in company culture. They subscribe.

**The sales moment**: And over months they start to learn about how they can create this glue as they scale their business. After they've been to your website a dozen times, you offer a free trial of your software. They're educated on culture now, they trust you as a brand, the odds of them giving it a go are high. And your sales process kicks into gear.

### *Content for the 30 per cent: (E)*
### *Not open to considering a solution*

This group is never going to come around. Perhaps it's ego, perhaps it's that their work situation doesn't allow for new ideas. Whatever it is, they are a group that would benefit from your offer but they will never buy.

The good news is that while this group isn't always obvious, inbound marketing won't cost you anything because they will rarely click on your content. Outbound marketing may cost you with this group but it's the price of appearing in front of the other groups.

# Part Two

# GETTING NOTICED: YOUR TRAFFIC CHOICES

This is the longest part of the book. With Part I laying the foundation of the trunk, you are now ready to move to the thick branches. Put on your gym clothes, put the phone on airplane mode and let's sweat through this. I'm going to teach you all the main ways to get your website noticed.

A quick preview of what the following six chapters will teach you:

- Chapter 5: Steal what works for your competition, and learn to be selective when finding the right channels (less is often more)

- Chapter 6: Search: how Google and other search engines send traffic

- Chapter 7: Social media: why *so* many companies are still doing social media ineffectively and how you can beat them

- Chapter 8: Paid: why this is the channel that unlocks your ability to scale

- Chapter 9: PR: the evolution of public relations from blunderbuss to sniper mode

- Chapter 10: Direct, email and dark social: the unglamorous tried-and-tested workhorses

# 5:

## FINDING TRAFFIC SOURCES

What you are about to read might make you feel uncomfortable if you have not spent much time with competitive business intelligence. The amount of data that you can use to reverse-engineer and uncover your competition's marketing activity might surprise you.

But you need to know that this intelligence technology exists and that it's likely being used against you in some form.

We'll also look at how to lead in your niche and spot the gaps in your marketing mix. Importantly, you'll also learn how to identify and stop wasting time and money on channels that devalue your brand.

Let's start with reverse engineering your competition.

## 5.1   The Ethos of Creativity and Original Ideas

Did you know that most of the top-of-the-chart hits on the radio, by artists like Britney Spears, Justin Bieber, Kelly Clarkson, Maroon 5, Rihanna, Taylor Swift and Katy Perry, are created by a few forty-something-year-old men and bald Norwegians?

What if I told you that there was a framework that identifies the right chord progression to make a hit song, by country? A formula that even instructs the colour of eye shadow that a performer should wear in different Asian regions? It's a precision model, as Jay Brown, a co-founder of Jay Z's label, said: 'You've got to have a hook in the intro, a hook in the pre, a hook in the chorus, and a hook in the bridge, too.'

These are all part of creating a commercially successful song and you can read all about it in *The Song Machine* by John Seabrook.

There are many similarities to the marketing framework most websites use to scale, from social-media culture by country to search-engine usage and copywriting tone. Oh, but what about creativity, you say? Yeah, you need that, but I advise letting creativity become the unique skin that covers the proven skeleton.

I don't mean to imply that this is easy. It's not. But the good news is that the framework exists and you can save time by following it.

The framework for website traffic is essentially all about adapting online the offline sales funnel, which can be traced back to 1898. A–I–D–A. We touched on it a few times now but let's bind it to memory. You'll be sick of AIDA by the end but you will remember it. *Muahahaha!*

**Attention**: Traffic Sources

**Interest**: First Visit

**Desire**: Repeat Visits

**Action**: Your website funnel's business objective

Creativity, like playing the blues, comes after you are well versed with the rules and framework that make it sound like the blues.

I recommend first seeking to understand what a solid website framework for your particular industry is by studying commercially successful competitors. Then your creativity can come in on the top of it. And at the attention level are the traffic sources, which is what we'll pull right apart.

## 5.2 How Do I Find Out What My Competition is Doing to Drive Traffic?

Let's do this the free way for now.

Install the following four extensions on your Google Chrome browser

- BuzzSumo: This will show you which pages are being shared on social media on any website.

- SimilarWeb: This will show you any website's traffic sources and estimate volume (rough estimates!).

- Ghostery: This will show you what marketing technology a website is running.

- SEOquake: This will show you overall SEO strength and who owns the domain and how long the site has been live.

Once these are installed, open up a blank Excel sheet and type a series of column headings:

- **Company Name**

- **Company URL**

- **Domain Date**: When the domain was bought. Find this by clicking the Whois on the SEOquake extension. Also check ownership if it belongs to the original owner.

- **Geography**: Check SimilarWeb's geography tab, write down the top three countries supplying traffic.

- **Indexed Pages**: This is the number of website pages that Google has record of. Use SEOquake to find this or just type *site:websitename.com* into Google. This tells you how big the site is.

- **Mobile**: Take the browser and make it as narrow as possible: did the website shrink to fit (i.e. is it responsive)? How does the website look on your mobile? Write *Yes* if it works well on mobile. Best to check on your actual phone too.

- **Backlinks**: Look at SEOquake and find the number of *external* backlinks that point back to the website, write the number here. I'm oversimplifying here but if this number is high it's indicative of strong SEO and an established brand.

- **Paid**: Cross-reference data from SimilarWeb and check SpyFu.com to see what ads they might be running on search engines. Assign a score from 0 (none) to 5 (lots).

- **PR**: Open the external-links tab in SEOquake and look through the backlinks. How many press and blogger links do you see? Score 0 to 5. This would show up as referral traffic in your analytics tool if you owned their website.

- **Search**: Reference SimilarWeb and SpyFu.com to gauge how much search traffic they might be getting. Also look at SEOquake's Diagnosis tab and have a look if their website is search-engine optimized to some level. Assign a score from 0 to 5.

- **Social**: Open up BuzzSumo and have a look how much their homepage has been shared. Or click visit BuzzSumo and pop their URL in and see what the top-five most-shared pages on their website have been in the last twelve months. Give a score from 0 to 5 and note which social-media channels are doing the shares.

- **Direct**: This is tricky to track, as direct traffic often swallows email traffic, untagged social traffic and all dark-social traffic. Regardless, open up SimilarWeb and assign a score from 0 to 5.

- **Main Traffic Sources**: Combining what you learned from paid/PR/search/social/direct and by looking at SimilarWeb's sources tab, write down the top one (or top three, if it's pretty even).

- **Traffic Estimate**: Pop in what SimilarWeb estimates for monthly visitors. I take their results as *very* rough estimates.

- **Ad Tech**: Click your Ghostery extension and write

down what advertising technology is listed here. This gives you clues as to what paid channels they are using.

- **Analytics and Tracking**: Click Ghostery and note what analytics they are using. If you see more than Google Analytics it should give you a clue as to what they are trying to measure.

- **Testing Software**: Click Ghostery and note if any testing software such as Optimizely is being used. If you see any testing software it's a signal that they take web traffic seriously.

| Company | URL | Domain Date | Geography | Indexed Pages | Mobile | Backlinks | Paid | PR | Search S |
|---------|-----|-------------|-----------|---------------|--------|-----------|------|-----|----------|
| Your Website | yourwebsite.com | 2008 | UK | 91 | Yes | 130 | 0 | 2 | 1 |
| Competitor A | competitora.com | 2013 | UK | 570 | Yes | 213 | 3 | 3 | 3 |
| Competitor B | competitorb.com | 2012 | USA, UK | 2,308 | Yes (sloppy) | 1,243 | 2 | 4 | 5 |
| Competitor C | competitorc.com | 2001 | AUS, UK, USA | 5,779 | Yes | 456 | 0 | 2 | 3 |
| Competitor D | competitord.com | 1999 | USA | 34 | No | 90 | 3 | 0 | 0 |
| Competitor E | competitore.com | 2006 | UK | 322 | Yes | 38 | 0 | 1 | 1 |

Right then. Are you still breathing or did this list cause pain in your membrane? Fear not, these areas will be explored in detail over the following chapters. But if after reading those chapters you still don't understand, I have a thirty-minute video I'm happy to send you that shows how I build an Excel list like this to help me pick the right traffic sources. Visit filipmatous.com/supplement and I'll send you a link.

Now with the top row's columns labelled, perform the research for three to seven competitors. If for some reason there isn't any obvious competition that is doing well online, audit websites that offer products that target the same personas as you do.

Also visit your competitors' social-media accounts and instead of looking at fan count, focus your attention on the amount of engagement each post they publish receives. That's a much better barometer of effective social-media use.

Finally, add your website to a row and audit yourself the same way.

### Important notes

SimilarWeb is the best traffic-estimating tool out there, in my experience, and also according to Moz, but it's not gospel. None of the traffic-estimating tools out there are that accurate.

If you do have budget to spend on this part of research I recommend you spend money on these tools:

- **SimilarWeb**: The pro account is a massive time-saver if you are going to be doing a lot of competitor research.

- **BuzzSumo**: The pro account is incredible at finding where your niche's content thrives, and comparing types of content that are topically popular: lists, video, infographics, how-to articles, what posts, and why posts.

- **SEMRush**: If you are going to be competing on AdWords and SEO, this tool is practically essential for finding out what ads your competitors are running and on what keywords, and finding their ad-copy history (if you find the same ad copy month over month = probably a profitable ad).

- **WhatRunsWhere**: This is the tool you want to have if you are trying to compete on display advertising.

- **Sysomos MAP**: This is much more expensive than any of the other tools, but should you need enterprise-level software to figure where to get not-paid-for traffic, this product is great. Simply Measured is also a choice I've heard great things about – but as I haven't used it I can't confirm.

## 5.3 Mobile Impact on Assist Interactions vs Last Interaction Traffic Channels

When Google describes the customer online journey, two things jump out at me that weren't so, back in 2014:

1. Mobile has changed everything due to *micro moments* – meaning all the times people get closer to buying something by researching things when they have a few minutes, perhaps while sitting on the toilet or commuting.

2. The number of people comfortable purchasing things through their mobile phone is, in many industries, *doubling year-over-year*.

This is a huge shift. Maybe you are like me and realized that having the Amazon app on your phone with its patented *1-click purchase* facility is rather dangerous. Seriously, how does Amazon have a patent on buying online with one click?! I digress. Mobile is changing the touch-points we used to expect back when desktops were the source of the vast majority of web traffic.

And those micro moments are summarized in four ways:

- I-want-to-know

- I-want-to-go

- I-want-to-do

- I-want-to-buy

People are slotting in these moments whenever a small pocket of time becomes available. They use these moments to check on products in stores, to look up someone right before a meeting, to fact-check, see if a flight is cheaper, to carry out due diligence on the company on the business card they just received or the restaurant they're about to enter.

Having a mobile website is not optional if you want to improve the odds of their visit during one of these micro moments being a pleasant one.

Now, tying this shift back to the purpose of this chapter, how do all these touch-points work with the traffic coming to your website?

Google categorizes these touch-points in two areas: Assists and Last Interactions:

- **Assist Interaction**: The touch-points at the beginning and middle of a journey to a lead or sale.

- **Last Interaction**: The final touch-point at the end of the journey, at the moment of purchase.

Search for 'Google customer journey', enter your industry, company size and country and Google will show you from its large data-set what traffic channels are suited at what stage.

This, mind, is just for online sales, but the traffic channels themselves are useful to understand, even if you are not selling anything directly online.

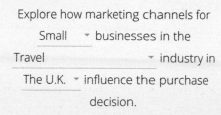

For more information, see: thinkwithgoogle.com/tools/customer-journey-to-online-purchase.html.

## 5.4   Ballparking Costs and Time Investment

Nothing is free. All traffic has a price.

It costs you time or it costs you money. Often it costs both.

I wish I had learned this lesson earlier in my career. If I were to pick between the paid-for traffic and the organic traffic that I traded my time for, I used to prefer investing time for results. But the volume of traffic was directly influenced by the amount of time I had. It was a foolish mindset. Achieving scale on my earlier projects would have happened much faster had I paid the right channels to boost traffic volume.

For example, have you ever heard someone say SEO is *free* traffic from Google? Truth is that it's often more expensive than the equivalent ad traffic on Google Search when you add up all the labour needed to make a page on your website rank for your desired term.

I encourage you to get comfortable with approaching all traffic sources with this mindset. All traffic costs.

Maybe you want to create content that goes viral? Well then you might not be paying that much to acquire traffic but you are paying in time or money to create outstanding content that attracts traffic.

It's surprising how many website owners fight against finding a healthy balance between investing time and money. I advise people to start with finding the right traffic sources regardless of what they cost and then figuring out how to pay for them.

## 5.5 Expect to Remove Channels that Don't Work

In 2012, I was moderating an afternoon session on web traffic and social media inside Microsoft's London headquarters. Among the bigger brand presentations, one small business presenter was showing her case study on using Twitter to draw awareness to her bakery. She explained her routine of spending twenty minutes a day growing a following on Twitter for the last six months. She said it was time well spent and that it grew her bakery.

Someone stood up in the crowd and asked her just how many sales she felt resulted from her investment of time. She said she wasn't sure but that at least a dozen people had mentioned something about Twitter in the store when buying baked goods. A *dozen* people?! If you have ever met me, you know my face betrays me, I have a hard time not showing what I'm thinking. Anyhow, I had to turn around so that the audience didn't see my unimpressed expression. I'm not sure why she was there in the first place as a case study.

The bakery maths: twenty minutes, five times a week, times six months, equals about forty hours of investment. And let's say her average order was £10, so £120 total benefit from forty hours of investment. Was her time worth £3 an hour?! Her social-media habits, should they increase in time-investment, could kill her business.

This is something I saw in the blog club too. People not being honest about what is working and what isn't. It's fine if you enjoy Twitter and call it a hobby – but it's not a real part of your marketing efforts if you can't trace it back to serious returns or at least effective customer service.

This is why Part III of this book will help you make the right decisions. Measurement isn't optional if you want to grow your business by getting your website noticed.

Next, we'll unpack an often confusing world: search-engine optimization. You'll want to understand this because, done right, it can provide quality traffic consistently.

# 6:

## ORGANIC SEARCH TRAFFIC

Back in 2007, when you searched 'Filip Matous' on Google you'd find a gay Czech porn star taking up a few of the first-page results. I still remember my surprise when I checked Google images for my classic Czech name. Then and there I got interested in changing what I saw when I searched for myself on Google, long before I had heard of the term SEO (Search Engine Optimization).

In this chapter we'll learn about search traffic that's branded, search traffic that comes around the final inter-action to a sale or lead, and search traffic that acts as an assist interaction. The other major thing you'll need to learn are the two sides of SEO and how search engines like Google judge a site: what's happening onsite (about 30 per cent of the game), and offsite optimization, mainly the backlinks pointing to your site (about 70 per cent).

Quickly, for clarification: it's called search-engine *opti-mization*, not *ranking*, which many think this is about. I won't only show you the basics of ranking for a keyword on Google, but focus on the optimization and how you do this for human eyeballs. You can have the best rankings, but if it doesn't look interesting to a human, you won't get the click.

Full disclosure: you need to know I've been involved with white-hat (clean, above-the-board tactics) and black-hat (somewhat dodgy tactics) SEO in the past, whether it was through SEO agencies I've hired or experiments that

I've run personally. I'm not here to pass judgement on what's right or wrong, rather I'm doing my job if I explain to you your options so you know how to make smart choices with SEO and what to advise a supplier. I'll add that I'm not an expert in SEO execution but I've spent years understanding the basics and hiring SEO consultants, and I know on a personal level some of the best in the biz.

Finally, I've been pulled in to manage reputational SEO clean-up jobs in the past. Businesses that bought cheap black-hat services back when they worked, and found themselves blocked from Google because they had 10,000 links pointing to their website from porn and gambling sites. I've also been the victim of black-hat SEO attacks, and have had two clients and one of my own sites in the past slammed with link injections for Cialis, Viagra and Wart medicine. One was so brazen that the first four inches of every page on my client's site was riddled with penis-enlargement links. You never forget the panic in the phone call or email when someone gets hit. It sucks and it's a stressful clean-up.

But I've also seen multiple family businesses grow their business off the back of SEO efforts. SEO isn't going to be dead for a long, long time.

## 6.1 What and Where Should I Rank For?

If you live in an English-speaking country, Google will be the most important search engine to worry about. Here in the UK, 90 per cent of searches occur on Google. In the USA it's 70 per cent. You can find the most popular search engine and the runner-up for your country by visiting: filipmatous.com/search-engines-by-country.

Common sense, but your efforts to rank should aim to please the primary search engine and possibly the runner-up.

### Keyword research: so what terms should you try to rank your website for?

So you want to increase traffic from Google and are comfortable with the process. How do you find which keywords to target?

#### *Branded-search keywords*

Really simple variations of your company name and the full names of all client-facing employees and management. If you are a company of one, your name might be the only branded term you worry about.

**Company name**: When creating your homepage, in many cases it's a good idea to ask your SEO supplier to make it rank for your company name – and nothing else. That might run counter to most of the advice out there, but I find this strategy allows you to attribute all organic search traffic coming to your website homepage as people searching for your brand.

Inside Analytics you'll find that Google hides almost all the keywords that bring traffic to your website by replacing the terms with 'not provided'. (This isn't the case with search ads.)

With a homepage that only ranks for your company name, you can measure the growth of interest in your brand by watching the increase in branded traffic hitting your homepage, even if analytics lists it as 'not provided'.

**Names**: Customer-facing employees and management should each have their own pages on your website. Too often I see team pages that lump everyone together. While it is good to list names and photos of everyone a customer or client might be looking up, not having individual pages for each person is a missed SEO opportunity.

When people have their own page on your website they can link to it from LinkedIn and any other relevant sites. Your sales team and management especially need this for people performing due diligence.

Once you have good optimization for everyone's name, you can see how much interest different people in your company are generating from the outside.* I reported on this for one agency and they found it amazing that they could see traffic spikes to their individual pages the day before, during, or after a new-client pitch meeting.

### Assist-interaction search keywords

These are the keywords that you want to rank for, which describe the challenges, interests and desires of your ideal personas rather than the exact services or products you sell. Keywords that match a part of the customer journey prior

---

* Really common names such as Jane Smith and the like may be impossible to rank for on their own, so make sure that their name + company name brings up their individual page and not the homepage.

to the final action. An SEO consultant and software like SEMRush come in handy for identifying keywords that you stand a chance of ranking for. These keywords will carry with them average monthly traffic estimates to help you identify which ones you should work to rank for. Some keywords are too hard to rank for so you want to know which ones make sense – otherwise you'll waste time.

Have a look at including keywords that your personas might be looking up long before they are ready to buy anything. For example, if you are selling rental villas for families in Puglia, Italy, you might want to create content and rank for 'family-friendly events in Puglia' and try to rank it in the country where your buyers are. If you can bring in traffic this way, you are on your way to introducing your brand at the interest level and then working on getting that repeat visit.

### At what stage is the market audience I'm trying to attract?

It's important to decide on keywords that match the stages of audience you are trying to attract, as we covered in 4.3:

- 3 per cent: (A) **actively**: Keywords which people who are actively searching might type in.

- 7 per cent: (B) **passively**: Keywords people might search for around your buying terms.

- 30 per cent: (C) **aware**: Keywords that talk about the problem solving or pleasure your offer provides.

- 30 per cent: (D) **unaware**: Keywords connected to

topics that your persona is interested in that have little to do with your final offer.

- 30 per cent: (E) **not open**: No keywords needed here, you'll never win these people over.

Note: Focus your efforts. A vacation client once had 15 per cent of their traffic coming from keywords related to 'hiking boots', which appealed to a much larger group of visitors than our target persona. Upon thirty minutes of research we could see that the traffic wasn't behaving like potential buyers. To keep the website focused on pleasing the right audience, we removed those pages altogether and put the effort into more closely related terms that targeted our personas.

### Final-interaction search keywords

These include:

- **Branded keywords**: but they also might add one of these words: 'contact', 'phone number', 'address'.

- **'On the tin' or buyer keywords**: what your personas search for during the 'actively' searching phase.

### Major search engines and internal search engines

If you've done your research you'll know which search engines are popular in your country, but it's important to note that there is another type of search engine that might also provide traffic back to your website – internal search engines:

- **Major search engines**: searches the whole internet for results.

- **Internal search engines**: only searches its own website or a small collection of related websites for results.

A few internal search engine examples:

- YouTube: Useful for thought-leadership and how-to videos that include a link back to your website.

- Amazon: If you are an author using a book to do lead-generation, optimizing to get found here with a link back to your site might matter.

- TripAdvisor: For restaurants, hotels and day events, ranking here with a link back to your site is crucial.

- Checkatrade: For tradesmen, an important place to rank and link back to their site.

## 6.2   Ranking Factors for the Gorilla (Google)

*'Oh Mum, we got hit sooo hard by the Panda update,' cries one SEO over the phone to his mother, trying to find comfort . . . 'What is it you do again, son?'*

Google keeps updating the ways they rank websites, evolving as Google rolls out search-algorithm updates. 'Algorithm' is a fancy word for the process Google uses to identify, order and display which web pages it believes best answer the searcher's query.

Some famous algorithmic updates:

**Panda** (February 2011, periodically updated): removes poor-quality content, but allows websites that are penalized to fix their problems in time for the next edition.

**Penguin** (April 2012, periodically updated): mainly to remove websites using black-hat spamming techniques to artificially rank higher.

**Exact Match Domain** aka EMD (September 2012, periodically updated): prevents weak websites from ranking just because they have their desired keyword(s) in the domain name.

**Hummingbird** (September 2013): adding more weight to the meaning in sentences instead of just individual words.

**Pigeon** (July 2014, not rolled out in every country): provides more useful local search results on Maps and standard Google search.

**Mobile-Friendly Update** aka *Mobilegeddon* (April 2015): boosts mobile-friendly results in Google's mobile results.

Back in 2010, Matt Cutts, former head of web-spam at Google, confirmed that over 200 ranking factors are used in ranking a webpage – and each factor could have fifty variations. So without trying to guess the details of some 10,000 different signals, let's learn the trends and key optimization considerations that aren't going away anytime soon.

## Onsite: how to optimize my site?

Let me give you some SEO advice so general it hurts:

> *Have a website that is easy to use*
> *that provides value to your market*

Yup, it's that hard. I'm not kidding; most sites screw up both of these things.

When considering the phrase 'easy to use' think about the whole funnel. Does your website display well on every popular device? Is your site fast enough to not irate people (three seconds or less)? Is the navigation simple and conventional? Will the visitor find what they need in three clicks or fewer? Do you use simple words and format to make your website easy to read, and by read I mean *scan*?

When it comes to value, are you really providing something that will make the visitor feel glad that they came to your site and gave you a few minutes of their time? Have you invested the time/money to make something that properly educates and/or appropriately entertains?

Here are eleven top onsite SEO considerations that aren't going out of style anytime soon:

1. **Value and engagement:** One purpose per page, one main keyword you want to rank for with preferably at least 500 words on the page – optimally around 2,000. The dwell time, page-scroll depth, comments and social shares all in one way or another impact SEO. These demonstrate *value*.

2. **Meta title:** After value, this on-page element usually matters the most. Have the keyword you want to rank for, ideally, at the front of the page title.

3. **Meta description:** Unique for each page? Although this doesn't influence the algorithm directly, it influences clicks because a good meta description is eyeball friendly and doesn't end in '. . .'

4. **Mobile friendly:** Your site will lose out on mobile traffic if this isn't done.

5. **Site speed:** Super important. Aim for two-second loads. Website uptime should be at 99.9 per cent and server location close to your core visitor's country. Content delivery networks (CDNs) on top of your hosting, site-caching, and website optimization (minifying images is a big one) can help achieve this. Test speed by using these providers; don't trust just one test as they will all vary a bit:

   • https://developers.google.com/speed/ pagespeed/insights/

   • http://www.webpagetest.org/

- http://yslow.org/
- http://tools.pingdom.com/fpt/
- The site-speed section inside Google Analytics

6. **Keyword saturation**: Should be found naturally in the title plus some secondary page titles (called H1 and H2), image title and alt description, and the keyword in the page URL if possible.

7. **No duplicate content**: Does your website use the same blocks of copy on multiple pages or is it found on different websites? Remove duplicates or you'll likely get penalized. You can use copyscape.com to check.

8. **Domain name**: generic top level domains (TLD) including .com, .net and .org are the most trustworthy and sought-after; country code top-level domains (ccTLD) such as .ca, .co.uk and .com.au can help rank you in a specific country but may limit global rank.

9. **Grammar**: Google's Panda update makes a negative impact on rankings for pages with poor grammar. Try using hemingwayapp.com to check readability level and clarity.

10. **Site architecture and usability**: How your pages are connected and laid out along with how your visitors navigate through these pages makes an impact. Never spare effort in setting up the foundation right so that your visitors and search engines have an easy time navigating your website.

**11. Structured markup**: The two you need to know:

- Open Graph (makes your site look good on social-media networks)

- Schema.org (makes your site look good on search engines)

    While this may just impact click-through rates, having done this extra microformatting will present your site better on search engines and social-media networks. If you don't have anyone technical on your team, try just using Open Graph – it's easier to grasp and still impacts how some things look on search engines.

Avoid at all costs:

- **Keyword stuffing**: Unnaturally overusing your keyword on a page. This worked many years ago but is a terrible idea now.

- **Recycling content**: This can be tempting to save time but it will cost you SEO strength. Each page should have original content or you need to use rel=canonicals (tells search engines where the original content lies).

- **Hyphenated domain names**: Can come across as spammy.

- **Too many outbound links**: Just use common sense; if you are blogging about something be careful how many external sites you are linking to.

- **Boring pages**: We've already learned about this but it really is too important not to repeat. Boredom has so many negative SEO impacts, don't publish unless it's likely to be interesting to your market.

## Offsite ranking factors: how to get links

So you have good onsite optimization, which is the first priority. Now you need to focus on the external part of SEO, essentially increasing your quality-backlink count. Think of the amount of quality backlinks as points Google references when ranking pages, and the more points you have the better you do.

Here are ten top offsite SEO considerations:

### 1. Your domain authority

The most important part of external SEO, a result of the quality of your external backlinks (links on other websites that point back to your site).

### 2. Link-diversity and relevancy

It's not enough to have links from other strong websites, you need to make sure that the niche the linking website ranks for is relevant to your niche. A cooking website would not receive many/any links from a car site, for example.

You'll want your backlink profile to be made of a mix of links from sites that complement your niche. And the timing matters too: there should be a steady growth of links pointing to your site over time. One rapid blast of links is a common sign that black-hat methods are in play and you might get sandboxed (Google removes you from search results). Slow, authentic and steady wins.

### 3. Number of linking root domains

'Root' means individual domains. Ten links from one website is much less valuable than ten websites each providing one link.

### 4. Anchor text

This is highlighted copy that links to a URL. Your anchor profile should be natural and include:

- Naked anchors: 'www.company.com/page-name'

- Branded anchors: 'company name'

- Generic anchors: 'click here'

- Descriptive anchors: 'Luxury cat food'

### 5. Natural-follow and no-follow link balance

No-follow links are tags that web masters can add to links that essentially tell Google not to count this / award a point. Lots of social-media sites also have no-follow links by default because people would spam the hell out of these sites if they gave follow links.

Naturally you should have a mix of these links. It's not good news if you have thousands of follow links and zero no-follow links because it looks like black-hat manipulation has been at play.

### 6. Internal links

Your site passes 'points', often called *juice*, from one page to the next too. Linking from pages on your website that have strong ranking to new pages you are trying to rank works.

Just be natural about it. Linking from all the pages on your website to one obscure page you are trying to rank is manipulative and may be punished.

### 7. Social-media links

While most of these are no-follow links, a high volume of social links is one of the signals Google uses to determine which pages are valuable.

### 8. Brand mentions

Your backlink profile should show a nice chunk of anchor text that uses your brand name. Google favours brands (even determining if the brand is associated with a tax-paying business and has a LinkedIn company page). If there isn't much online showing people talking about your brand then Google assumes you don't have a brand worth talking about.

### 9. Contextual links

The actual location of your link matters. The most potent are links inside an article, close to the top.

### 10. Tiers

Black-hat and white-hat SEOs, along with all the shades of grey, often map out their link profile in terms of tiers. While to this point we've been talking about tier-one backlinks, i.e. the links that point to your website, let's learn about tier-two links.

Let's say you have a PR agency that is landing you coverage in online press. They've managed to also get a link or

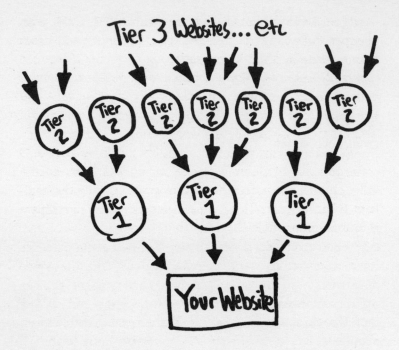

two inside these articles that point to your website. Tier-two links are links that point to that PR article, *not* to your website.

- Tier 1: Website *b* → your website (→ = link)

- Tier 2: Website *c* → website *b* → your website

- Tier 3: Website *d* → website *c* → website *b* → your website

And just as your website wins by having more points than a competitor, so do these articles. SEOs often boost tier-one link strength by building tier-two links back to tier one. And this can go on, it's very common to have three tiers in competitive spaces, sometimes even more.

If you decide to dabble in black-hat, NEVER, EVER push cheaper links back to your website. Distance them from your website by pointing to tier-two or tier-three if they are especially rubbish links. It's almost impossible to remove poisonous links if they point directly to your website and I've heard of brands starting from scratch on a new domain because their link profile is beyond repair.

It's worth noting that, while controversial, negative SEO – the practice of slamming competitors with poor-quality links on purpose – does happen in some competitive markets. If karma exists, I sure hope it gets those that participate in this awful practice.

Note: I can't wait for the day when *all black-hat* becomes ineffective, but it's just disingenuous to pretend that some manipulation isn't working well today. Many prestigious brands out there, upon examination of their link profile, have black-hat manipulation a tier or two away. But I moved away from black-hat for one major reason: long-term success doesn't need to be built on spam. Put your efforts into white-hat and you'll reap rewards long term and stay safe. Plus, that karma thing . . .

Below are some modern black-hat methods, which your competitor may be using:

- In PR: While the practice is hush-hush, the economics of being a journalist or editor often get muddy when an SEO is paying you a couple of thousand to write an article that includes a link. Various shades of grey are found here.

- Link brokers: Private networks of people who sell links on high-domain websites exist. These links can cost hundreds or thousands of pounds apiece.

And they work. You won't find this information publicly available, but if you are in the industry, you'll come across connections.

- Comment spam: Oh how I hate thee. I had one client who had 50,000 spam comments on their website and wondered why they were not ranking for anything online. When I brought in a supplier to remove these, the weight of these links made the CMS unusable. Nightmare to fix. If you have a blog make sure you don't have comment spam, it can quickly drop your rankings.

But with every passing year, more and more SEOs are keeping it white-hat because the long-term benefit outweighs the short-term gain of black-hat.


### Specific SEO: local, video, news, ecommerce

For some websites, getting specific with what you want to rank for means picking specific parts of a search engine to rank. These include:

- **Local**: If you have a business that relies on foot traffic, appearing well in Google Maps might be very important. Know that part of the SEO industry specializes just in local search. There are things you can do to optimize for this. A start is using Moz Local to clean up and make sure you are using the same address format across the web, so that you show up more in local searches.

- **Video**: YouTube isn't the only way to rank in

Google. You can customize your web page to show up in video results. A good place to start on this is reelseo.com, or if you are using WordPress, Yoast's video plugin is great too.

- **News**: If you have timely, newsworthy content, appearing in Google and Yahoo News can drive a potent amount of traffic (FYI, it will be close to a 100 per cent bounce-rate). Again there are ways to optimize your website for this. You'll need to meet the requirements here: https://support.google.com/news/publisher/answer/40787, and then you'll need to submit your website for approval here: https://partnerdash.google.com/partnerdash/d/news.

- **Ecommerce**: If you are in ecommerce and want to get listed in Google Shopping, you'll need to do some Schema.org work and prepare your site to meet Google's requirements. Search for 'Google Merchant Center' and follow the rabbit hole.

# 7:

## SOCIAL TRAFFIC

**A quick summary of the main channels and how to think about social and first-mover advantage**

– Suggest someone comes, has a look at the epic queues and utter chaos around the toilets! Only one set open on statn, madness!!

*– Hi, [name removed], apologies and thanks for letting us know. Should be back to normal. Hope you have a good weekend. Best, Filip*

– Thank you. I am not exaggerating – there was a queue of at least 200 schoolgirls plus everyone else. Open the other loos!

*– Have been told the toilets were temp closed as someone stuffed large items down the toilet pans, blocking the evac system :(*

Have I got your attention or what?! This is an actual *thrilling* tweet conversation we dealt with at Evergreen Reputation when we were handling social media for a massive train station in London. When I hear the hopeful excitement of young people wanting to work in social media I chuckle. Yes, social is interesting at times, but it's lots of work, you deal with plenty of negativity, and it's often hard to show ROI.

'Meet Filip, he's a social-media guru . . .' I heard this often around 2009–2012 when being introduced and it made me cringe. I know it was meant well but I'm a loser who dislikes being called a guru. Or ninja. Or rockstar . . .

I'm none of those cool descriptions, even if I wish I were – and never have the other people in social media whom those words were used about actually lived up to expectations. Often I felt the word 'clown' was more accurate. I prefer how my friend Paul usually introduces me: 'Filip knows some stuff about the interwebz'. That's more accurate, as 'some' implies just how much stuff I have no idea about.

So what stuff can I pass on to you about social media to help get traffic onto your website? Well first, and thankfully, social media is no longer new and sexy. It's taken its rightful place in the marketing mix, the hype is almost gone, and it's being measured against other traffic channels. What this chapter will do is break down how to think about the popular platforms and how to use an acceptable amount of risk when trying for first-mover advantage while using new social-media networks.

Let's also get this out of the way: having success on any of these social platforms comes down to understanding the business model behind each platform, playing to it, and empathizing with the audience. Each of these platforms has its own culture and etiquette, and the fastest way to lose is to just blast each platform with the same content and tone.

My goal for you in this chapter is not to use all these channels, but to be selective on picking one to three channels that fit your niche, and to help you get into the trenches to learn the culture and process.

Let's start with the monster.

## 7.1   Facebook

I say monster because of a few facts:

1. The majority of 2016 online advertising budgets are going to mobile. (Source: http://www.investopedia.com/articles/investing/071315/mobile-ad-competitors-facebook-vs-google.asp).

2. In 2015, Google and Facebook together represented the majority of mobile-ad spend, and it's not going to be a shock if Facebook ends up taking more mobile-advertising revenue than Google at its rate of growth.

3. Facebook (over 1 billion daily users) owns Instagram (400 million users uploading 80 million photos per day) and WhatsApp (over 1 billion users) – the data-communication and advertising options between these networks are just getting started.

4. Apple iOS9 blocks Google's ads, yet allows Facebook because it's in-app.

5. Facebook is a real threat to YouTube's mobile video dominance. And mobile video is exploding; many businesses won't be able to compete without it in the near future.

So that's fact mixed with my predictions, and while some people are fasting from Facebook or leaving altogether, for most, it's a compulsive habit to check multiple times each day to get a dopamine hit.

### The main pros and cons of Facebook for driving traffic back to your website

*Pros*

- The majority of people with a smartphone use Facebook.

- For every age group, it's a popular social network, even for teenagers, despite huge growth on Instagram, Twitter and Snapchat. Whoever your persona is, you'll find them here.

- Targeting on Facebook is profile-based and makes for great assist interactions.

- Video ads, if they are entertaining, are starting to work really well here.

- Retargeting options are glorious here. Someone visits your website and then sees some of your website content on their news feed. Great for increasing brand touch-points.

*Cons*

- Usually not the best network for a final assist.

- Not a great fit for corporate messages, as it must be entertaining to some degree.

- Tight rules on what kinds of external pages you can and cannot link to in promotions.

- Organic reach for fan pages is rarely worth doing if you don't have budget.

### Example: growing a fan page to push traffic back to a website

It's Friday night and I'm chillin' at Sam's place. Instead of enjoying the evening, we're staring at his laptop and battling rapid-fire Facebook spam. (Yes, I know my life sounds *soo* cool.) Every ten seconds or so our client's Facebook account is getting spammed with people trying to win a freebie that we're giving away. We're not achieving our client's goal, don't know how to make it stop, and we're entirely responsible.

Background: For a couple of years we managed the social-media channels for one of London's main train stations. One of its most popular direct-travel destinations was Paris. The station saw hundreds of thousands of people walk through it every week and it had many high-end restaurants, bars and shops that made it a place people would visit, even if they weren't using the trains.

Our goal: station brand marketing. To use Facebook to make people aware of the things you could do in the station. To make it a destination. We measured success by the volume and sentiment (positive vs negative) of brand-mentions each month.

When we started on Facebook we tested many different ways of getting attention and the only thing that really began to work was posting pictures of things in and around the station. We'd search for and share people's photos from the station. We'd share historic photos. There were pianos there that anyone could play and those got loads of attention online. Every Christmas a giant themed Christmas tree would go up in the centre of the station and the number of photos online would explode. Essentially, our best use of time was amplifying other people's photos and adding some of our own – with this we'd reach hundreds of thousands of people online each month. Then when we linked back to the website with information about some event, we'd use a similar style and traffic would flow to the website.

What didn't work was anything salesy, and we tried many different approaches. We tried promoting food from the restaurants and engagement would drop. BUT when we used a photo that showed the food AND the station in the background, engagement would go up. When we tried coupons, engagement dropped. But when we promoted 2-for-1 champagne with a picture of the long champagne bar, engagement increased. Notice a trend? Everything had to show off the station.

The worst was freebies on Facebook, and we stopped this after two horrific attempts. Following an offer going live, people would enter and loads of other people and software programs would hammer the offer. Yet hardly any of these people wanting the free stuff matched the audience who would visit the station.

## Formats that work for driving traffic

So what works overall on Facebook?

### Photos

If you have real photos that are circumstantially relevant to your brand, use them. Avoid stock images or overly polished images. These rarely work. Also, if you are planning on using paid promotion (you should do if your brand is a fit for Facebook) then make sure your photos have less than 20 per cent text, otherwise Facebook will block your promotion.

Instagram photos integrate okay . . . because Facebook is fine with trading traffic between the two networks. But I suggest you upload content to each platform individually because all of them have different styles and functions. Automation isn't worth the decrease in engagement.

### Text-only posts

Facebook allows very limited formatting but it does allow paragraph breaks. Big blocks of copy don't work. Usually short messages are the best.

### Video posts

You can use YouTube, Vimeo and other video providers, but for the greatest reach, use Facebook's proprietary video hosting. Think about it, why would Facebook want to give traffic to a competitor?

Vertical video: why use 25 per cent of the screen for video when you can use all of it? Vertical video makes sense for mobile campaigns, so have a play with it to see how it works for your brand. For a sneak peak at where it's all going, look at how Snapchat uses vertical video.

### Analytics

Let's talk about the traffic that flows from Facebook back to your website. While the analytics that measure the traffic that stays on your fan page have depth, the traffic that flows back to your website will usually show up as 'Facebook' in your analytics, but there's a more thorough way. Try to use UTM tracking to measure each effort. In the third part of the book I'll show you how to do this without adding a load of time to your workflow.

You can also add Facebook conversion pixels to your website. These help fill in a lot of the unknowns in Facebook's analytics. Google 'Jon Loomer': he's one of the best in the Facebook marketing space.

## 7.2   Twitter

Twitter has a learning curve higher than most of the other channels, especially if you are using it to push traffic back to your website. Which might sound silly because it's 140 characters, right? But to get actual engagement takes, in my opinion, just as much skill as Facebook.

One massive point to start: brand-driven accounts often do far worse with reach than individual accounts.

If it's in your business's interest to be on Twitter, try to have your company's thought leader, instead of a logo, head the campaigns on Twitter. If you must lead with a logo, make sure that the bio includes who is doing the tweeting. If there are multiple people tweeting then make sure to have them add their initials or name to the tweet if they are doing @ replies.

Short primer on Twitter:

- Update: Can be up to 140 characters, can include images or a thirty-second video.

- @ replies: These are tweets that begin with an '@' – only the person(s) tagged in the tweet will see the tweet on their timeline.

- DM: Direct message, meaning private messages.

### The main pros and cons

*Pros*

- Great place for intelligent content marketing.

- Clean advertising interface for paid targeting: my favourite tactic, marketing to the customers and fans of competing brands.

- Retargeting: People visit your website, then they can see you in their Twitter newsfeed (I suggest content over sales as sales messages on Twitter bomb hard).

- One of the best ways to get on the radar of industry influencers in your space (most authors, leaders and journalists are found there).

- Great for customer service.

- Traffic coming to your website from Twitter is generally quality.

*Cons*

- Learning curve: It's easy to be completely ignored.

- Momentum: There's an etiquette that you need to understand to have any traction. Also having a solid follower-to-following ratio makes an impact on people. I try to get established accounts to have ten followers for every one person they follow.

- Images on Twitter get cropped on different devices in different ways. This means that if you use images containing copy, you have to play with large margins or people might not be able to read what is on the image.

- Tweet outside of your core topic and engagement plummets.

Warning: **Don't ever buy fake followers** in order to make yourself look more influential. People who use Twitter on a daily basis know a gamed account when they see one. It's off-putting and erodes brand trust. I say this because I've seen it too many times, seen people get turned off from fake accounts, and have been on the clean-up-job side where I have to manually remove the fake followers. It isn't pretty. Five dollars for one thousand followers? Don't do it.

## Example: Pushing traffic organically

It can be uncomfortable to audit your tweets, but one podcast I've been helping lately tweeted about eight times a day and published one new episode once a week. When we looked through the tweets, they were comprised of two kinds: (*a*) episode announcements, about 15 per cent and (*b*) industry updates, about 85 per cent. The thinking was that (*a*) would drive traffic back to the website and (*b*) would grow the account followers.

Adding bit.ly (a popular URL shortener that includes tracking) to all the tweets with links we could see where people were clicking, we found that (*a*) drove 90 per cent of the clicks, and (*b*) drove 10 per cent of the clicks, and those were not clicks to our website.

Then when we looked at followers and losses, we could see that the higher volume of industry tweets actually didn't grow the account and were responsible for the majority of people un-following the account.

Why? Because people followed the podcast account for one reason: to get (*a*). To get updates when the next episode came out. They didn't want (*b*) because it was recycled news from other industry sources they already followed: (*b*) added noise to their feed.

Action: We stopped the tweets about the industry, re-formatted the updates about the show to include images, and relied on bit.ly to track how much traffic it was sending back to our website. The Twitter account now published 15 per cent of the tweets it used to publish, and the noise was completely cut.

Results: Organic-follower count-rate rose, clicks through to the website increased and, importantly, the thirty minutes a day spent by the team member in charge of creating the industry tweets was removed, allowing the social-media manager to use time more effectively.

One more thought: One topic per account. This lesson applies to pretty much every online asset you might have, but is crucial for Twitter if you are using it to drive traffic back to your website.

When I was involved with the social-media setup of the City of London Corporation, they made the smart choice to split up topics by handles. So if they were talking about Tower Bridge, the tweets came from @TowerBridge. If the Lord Mayor of London was tweeting it came from @City LordMayor. Information connected to Hampstead Heath would come from @CityCorpHeath. Announcements from the City of London Corporation would come from @City ofLondon. You get the drift: if you have an account, make sure that people can describe in one sentence what they expect to read if they follow that account. Then stick to that topic.

## Adding a Twitter card to your website

If you are pushing traffic from Twitter back to your website, invest the hour or less of labour to get a Twitter card on your website so that any time someone shares your website, it looks good on Twitter. The main benefits:

- **Consistent title, description and image**: Rich media attached any time you or someone else shares a page from your website on Twitter no matter what they write as their tweet copy.

- **Attribution**: Even if someone doesn't mention your Twitter handle and just shares a page on your website, Twitter will add your handle to the rich media – which can result in more Twitter followers.

- **Analytics**: Allows you to track how many people flow from Twitter to your website.

- **Remarketing**: Allows you to create remarketing lists from those people that visit your website.

- **Mobile**: Provides more information about your page and takes up more space on the feed causing more clicks.

So many advantages to setting this up. For each page on your website you can choose one of these cards:

- **Summary card**: Title, description, thumbnail, and Twitter account attribution.

- **Summary card + Large Image**: Just like the summary card but replaces the thumbnail with a large featured image.

- **App card**: A card to detail a mobile app and option to download.

- **Player card**: A card to provide video or audio.

Go to https://cards-dev.twitter.com/validator once you have done this to test how it will look.

### Analytics

The main thing you should be looking for is the engagement rate by tweet and patterns in the types of tweets that do well. Do more of those and cut the ones that are not performing.

Also have a look month by month at what the top tweets were and how many tweets you sent vs how many followers you gained.

What Twitter doesn't do well is show your traffic and follower-count over months and years. I recommend tracking that with third-party social-media tracking software such as sproutsocial.com and referencing the traffic Twitter provides with Google Analytics / Adobe Analytics to get a better understanding of how Twitter impacts traffic and conversions.

## 7.3   LinkedIn

LinkedIn is similar to Facebook in that you can get some traffic results organically – but it really opens up once you start paying to amplify your content.

It's a platform that's best suited for business-to-business content marketing. The best performing method I've tried for pushing traffic from LinkedIn back to your website is by using sponsored company updates.

So what do you need to know about getting traffic from LinkedIn? Let's first talk about the most ineffective way:

Leaving a flaming brown bag of poop on someone's doorstep.

That brown bag is showing up on someone else's platform and dropping a link to a page on your website. If you or one of your team says something along the lines of 'I'm going to my network and blasting that link everywhere', stop them from dragging your brand down.

Blasting your link everywhere is inconsiderate to your network and it doesn't get you many, if any, clicks. Plus it could get you reported for spamming. The worst is joining a LinkedIn group, showing up just to drop your link, and then running away. It's an effort to distract people's attention from the group discussion and onto your site. Do you think any group moderator is going to like that? You're having a classy party and some unknown dude or dudette shows up and yells 'Look at me, check this out!'

Seth Godin calls it 'permission marketing'. If you want to get some attention you had better offer loads of value first, and gain the permission to get more attention. If you want to get traffic from a group, actually engage with the group dozens of times. Then when it actually makes sense to include a link from your website that offers value to the discussion, it will be appropriate and should send traffic.

Same with your LinkedIn updates. If all you are doing is showing up, dropping a link, and walking away . . . let me channel Seinfeld's Soup Nazi after not keeping to the rules of engagement: 'No traffic for you!' But if you are commenting and engaging with others, actually being interested and connecting, then it makes sense if once in a while you post some content from your site.

Even LinkedIn wants to stop bleeding traffic to outside websites. It therefore incentivizes content creators by giving them an option of writing full blog posts right on LinkedIn. It will alert your network to these posts much better than it will an update with an external link.

### The main pros and cons

*Pros*

- It's some of the best quality B2B traffic you can get.

- It's hard for spammers to make any noise.

- The traffic that comes from LinkedIn often spends a decent amount of time on your website.

- When people engage with your posts, those engagements show up in the feeds of their network and you can get some really good engagement going outside of your own network – resulting in traffic.

- It makes a lot of sense to link to your website bio or homepage in the Contact section.

- It's the best platform for knowing specifically whose radar you are on.

*Cons*

- It's the most expensive social network if you are paying for exposure. Five dollars per click is common.

- The formatting and tagging options are not keeping pace with other social networks.

- Besides sponsored company updates, most of the other advertising offers (email and text-only ads) just don't do that great.

- It takes a lot of work to get traffic organically and your profile better look professional and full. Perhaps this should be listed as a positive . . .

### Profile-link drops

If you are going to try to get a click back to your website I recommend combining a short sentence with the link and an image that contextually makes sense. These get the best click-through rates, in my experience. Having a face in the image helps too.

You can do text updates, photo updates and full-post updates. Make sure, as with links on other social networks, to tag your traffic with UTM.

### Group-page-link drops

Pick your battles, make one or two groups the place you take time to engage and lose the title of stranger. Once you do, if you drop a link that makes sense into the conversation it won't be weird.

### Company-page-link drops

Often these pages get checked by people who want to scope out your company during due diligence, but they don't send much traffic to your website unless you do sponsored updates.

Targeting example: When I was finding an audience for *Marketing Not Magic* episodes, the target personas were London-based business owners and partners of companies of between twenty and fifty people. LinkedIn was able to zero in on this audience and provide me with 21,000 people to present my video content to. And targeting can go a lot deeper.

### LinkedIn analytics

These show you the actual people engaging with your content. The sales navigator is worth the monthly cost if you plan to spend a decent amount of time on LinkedIn each week.

You can see how many people click your links on Linked In, but again, you'll really want to take care of tagging up the links with UTM if you want accurate tracking in your website analytics.


## 7.4   Instagram

Instagram isn't an easy social platform to drive website traffic from – unless you are paying for ads. Regular posts on Instagram don't allow links and the only place you can put a link is in the bio of your account.

HOWEVER. If you have a product or service that photographs well, don't rule it out. Even though the volume of traffic is low, if people resonate with your photos and take the extra effort of going through your bio link, the traffic will be warm.

At Evergreen, Sam did this well for a classy hotel bar in London, using photos of fancy cocktails being made in the bar, photos of events, and he liked and regrammed (shared) some of the other people's photos of their time in the bar. This got a good fan base and when it came to announcing special events, fans would be informed and some would use the link to go to the website to find out more.

With Facebook and Instagram merging advertising platforms, if you have some budget to use on Instagram you can add all the links you please. But still make sure you understand the etiquette on Instagram and fit the medium.

Some thoughts about Instagram:

- Good engagement, noticeably more than on Twitter

- Popular and growing network

- Integrates with Facebook

- Hard to push website traffic

- Haven't found any convincing cases for promoting anything B2B

## 7.5   YouTube and Video

It's about two months from the biggest day of the year for a client. They are hosting an event on emotional intelligence for management; the speakers and flights are booked, the central London venue that needs about 400 attendees to be profitable is down-paid, the website has been live for months, accepting ticket purchases at around £500 a piece (there were a couple of ticket options), but one important thing is missing: attendees.

The email-marketing team wasn't converting to traffic or sales. They were using this funnel:

*Direct email → event sales page*

The LinkedIn email-marketing package wasn't moving the needle either:

*LinkedIn emails → event sales page*

So it was time to break out this funnel:

*Traffic source → content → YouTube retargeting → event sales page*

YouTube played a crucial role in both the original traffic source and especially in the retargeting role.

At the initial-traffic-source level we used:

- LinkedIn-sponsored updates to attract the personas who matched the event

- Twitter promotions to fans of the speakers at the event

- YouTube video pre-roll ads in front of videos of the speakers and also in front of videos resulting from 'emotional intelligence' related term searches*

It ended up being a combination of LinkedIn-sponsored updates and Twitter that generated the volume of traffic at the top of the funnel. And YouTube retargeting brought

---

* Pre-roll videos are the short videos you usually skip in front of the video you want to see. The trick in getting those videos to work is context. If the pre-roll starts and the video has lots to do with the video you are waiting for, many people will actually let the video play. If the context is wrong, *'le skip'*.

people back to the website for a repeat visit. When we tracked the average time to purchase it was between ten days and a month. YouTube was a helpful medium to get people increasingly interested in the event. They'd already got to know the event brand at the cold-traffic stage. And now they were warm. The YouTube video added to the touch-points and the traffic flowing from YouTube to the website showed quality because of the pages that traffic visited.

YouTube was the best late-assist to final interaction. We filled the venue with the majority of tickets sold in the last thirty days, and I'm not sure how close we would have got without all the streams of traffic and the YouTube video for the hat-trick.


## Passing 100 views: getting proper distribution so the investment in video pays off

Say you spend a long time planning, filming and editing a video. Because of all the effort, you imagine that you'll put it out there and people will watch. Now that it's live you look at the statistics and join the majority of online videos: under 100 views. Happy-balloon goes 'pop'. Deflated.

So how can you use video to drive traffic back to your website – when so many videos fail to even get views, let alone clicks? By being ruthless with what is interesting and what's boring – and putting money into promotion once you are sure that it's good enough.

Unless you have a network of what Kevin Kelly, the founding editor of *Wired* magazine, calls 'a thousand true fans', your market won't find your video without distribution. To get distribution, you might:

- seed your video with influencers (perhaps by involving them in the video)

- make a video so interesting that it goes viral (a-ha-ha-ha, this is *sooo* hard)

- pay YouTube, Twitter or Facebook to put your video in front of your market

- use PR to get your video embedded in established publications with an audience that matches

The best ROI is usually from paying to get distribution because you can fine-tune it as you go, and stop efforts that don't have any results. But you have to market validate that your video is actually interesting to your persona.

### Is my video boring? Measuring audience-retention and drop-off points

Uncovering the percentage of people that make it through various parts of the video is essential for deciding if your video is validated by the market before you pour money into getting more attention. This is where audience-retention analytics come in. You can break down your video into three parts: the nose, the body and the tail.

- **The nose:** The start, perhaps the first five seconds. Of course it starts at 100 per cent, but if this drops fast over these seconds then you can conclude their first impressions made the viewer decide it wasn't for them.

- **The body:** The mass of your video. There will be a gentle downward slope, but look for any sudden drops – they indicate that something in the video just isn't working. And if the slope is aggressive, your video probably isn't suitable for the audience.

- **The tail**: Where the video is wrapping up. It's natural that people abandon the video here as they feel they have consumed the good stuff and are done. But if you have a call to action at the end of the video make sure it comes in fast before the tempo is gone if you want people to see it and take action.

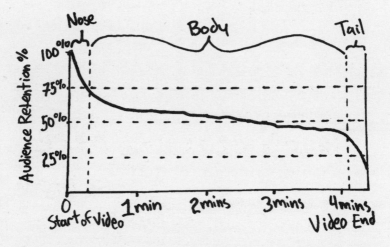

Some good reading from Alyce Currier and Ezra Fishman at Wistia: http://wistia.com/library/understanding-audience-retention.

It can be hard to admit a video isn't working, especially if you are closely attached to a video project, but you must open yourself to the fact that your video just might not be good enough and use the feedback to improve.

YouTube, Vimeo Pro and Wistia all provide this data.

### Some distribution techniques

#### *YouTube*

Pre-roll allows you to place your video in front of:

- your competitors' videos
- videos that match relevant search terms
- hand-picked videos that you'd like to appear in front of (I recommend picking ten relevant, popular videos)
- Review videos

It also allows retargeting – if people have been to your website, you can get your video on their next YouTube session.

This is cheap traffic with lots of ad inventory, and works better than the other options YouTube provides. Right now most views cost between 7 and 15 pence. This will go up as more advertisers use YouTube.

LinkedIn and Twitter also have the ability to stream your YouTube video right inside their platform.

### Facebook

Facebook allows you to target specific types of people, and this can be very effective. Expect many people not to have sound turned on whilst surfing Facebook, so try to make your video work without sound, at least at the beginning. And upload your video to Facebook directly; you'll have more reach than if you use YouTube.

Tip: be mindful of video advertising on mobile; if people don't know you, you might want to set the settings to only advertise to mobiles that are using Wi-Fi. Data caps might cause terrible engagement.

Another method that works very well with distribution and doesn't cost ad budget is video interviews with people with larger networks in your industry. If you can make a great video about someone or their company, it's predictable that they'll share the video with their network, which brings you a fresh new audience. And it's warmer traffic, as the reputation that the person in the video has will transfer to some degree to your website.

### Call to action: taking the viewer's attention from the video and continuing their journey onto your website

What is the next thing you want people to do after watching your video? Click to visit a specific page on your website?

If you are using YouTube you can connect your website

to your YouTube account and put annotations right in the video that people can click on and that will take them to a specified page on your website.

If you are distributing video through Facebook it's a little harder, but just put the link in the copy around the video.

You should avoid not having any action at the end of the video. This is the best time to invite people to do something, as they've given you their attention and perhaps have more trust in you.

### Videos already on your website

One client who sells software has a four-minute introduction video we produced (hat-tip to Ketan at Amoveo) sitting on the software sales page. It is used on the page to build trust by introducing the viewer to the people behind the software, allowing them to hear testimonials by some of its users, and showing off the software benefits.

It gets about 2,000 views a year, that's five views a day, which might sound low, but those are people actively checking out the product or doing due diligence. These viewers usually watch the whole video – solid audience retention. The video's purpose is to help the viewer to make their decision on the software and give the edge over competing brands.

Have a look at Wistia (paid-for video hosting). It does a great job of making a clean CTA on your website video.

Not all videos need to be seen by loads of people. Some videos are built for the Interest or Desire level, which should carry far fewer views than a video built for getting attention from a cold audience.

## Analytics

As we learned, never skip tracking audience-retention, and uncovering the drop-offs during the nose, body and tail of your video.

How did people find your video?

If you are organically sharing your video, it's important to note the referral traffic. YouTube can show you just how people found your video and the websites that sent traffic to you. Look for 'traffic sources' when you are signed into your YouTube account. Vimeo has something similar; don't use a video host without this feature.

No matter what you are using to host your video, look for the ratio of people that watch your video vs those who click through to your website, if you are trying to prove that your video pushes interested traffic.

Video is already big for pushing web traffic and it's going to get massive for companies in the future. Quality levels will keep going up and people will expect to see video about what you offer.

## 7.6    Other Social Networks

### Pinterest

Take a look at the research from the University of Minnesota's Pinterest Study and see if your website is a match to the most popular categories on Pinterest. Visit filipmatous. com/pinterest-research and it will redirect you there.

If it makes sense to market your website on Pinterest, invest time in learning two things:

- **Rich pins**: Find out how to get your website articles optimized for rich pins as these have the ability to send a great volume of traffic back to your site. These rich pins add extra information to each pin, similarly to how Twitter cards add extra information to each tweet.

- **Pinterest's advertising platform**: It's open to companies of all sizes and just like the other social platforms, invest budget here if you are able to match your website content to one of the popular categories. Format it into a rich pin that fits Pinterest's etiquette; you'll likely add a quality stream of traffic to your website.

### Google+

One red flag that indicates to me that a website owner doesn't measure traffic ROI is a link to Google+ on their homepage. I've checked at least a hundred different brands and *none* of them had anything worthwhile going on Google+. It's a sign of some guru yelling that the organization concerned should be on every platform. And now the slow death: Google announced it's splitting Google+ into streams and photos. The only thing that seems to have any traction are the useful but awfully laggy Google Hangouts.

The only thing I recommend Google+ for? When you post a new article or blog post, post it on Google+: it will immediately get the page indexed (this means it is eligible to be found by people on Google search). Or don't. You aren't missing anything really.

## 7.7  First-Mover Advantage and the Future

But.

What about Snapchat?

Even six months ago I wouldn't have thought about including this social network in this book, as I just didn't get the hype.

It's now at 200 million users and growing, outside the original 13- to 23-year-old demographic. Big consumer brands are signing up and content-marketing. If you want to see where vertical video is going, spend fifteen minutes signing up and looking at the stories section of the app. Even if your teenage daughter laughs at you for having it on your phone.

I'm not going to pretend I have it figured out, but I will say that I agree with the observations of fellow online marketers like Gary Vaynerchuk: Snapchat's approach to attention stands out. Instead of being about impressions (let's be candid, a totally worthless metric), it's about short, live content that people focus their attention on because it disappears after viewing.

This might have a big impact on other social-media attention.

## Other networks

So we didn't talk about some of the other social networks, like Periscope, Vine, Xing (aka German LinkedIn), Tumblr, MeetUp, etc. While there may be a good social network that helps you push traffic back to your website, I recommend keeping this mindset when deciding whether or not a social network is worth your time over some other use of your time:

1. Does the network have a good chunk of people who fit my persona?

2. Can I use the platform to push traffic back to my website?

3. How much time do I have to give this every week for it to gain momentum?

4. If I do use this network, where am I taking the time from?

You've got lots to gain by being ahead of the competition when it comes to getting on a relevant social network. The ability to get a jumpstart on a platform combined with low costs of advertising can make this a savvy move for cheap traffic. Just as the costs of Facebook advertising keep going up, with every new social platform the initial costs are usually far lower than what they get to once the network matures and there is high demand from a load of advertisers.

Okay, so in the next chapter we're going to go over a bunch of different ways you can pay for traffic that gets people on your website. But I urge you to seek opportunities to blend these two chapters together: when social has paid budget behind it, *oh baby* . . . This is probably my favourite type of traffic, because it takes skill, content and strategy to pull off. It's something many competitors just won't take the time to iron out.

# 8:

## PAID TRAFFIC

This is usually the topic that can take marketing and sales generation from random to consistent fire hose. It's also feared by many small companies because they don't know how to get into paying for traffic without losing money.

Note: For this chapter I had Luke Alley looking over my shoulder. Luke has managed over £12 million in spend across Google Adwords, BingAds, Facebook and other platforms. Awarded Microsoft's Most Valuable Professional for his work in PPC, he's a rising young gun.

Here's the truth: when you start in paid traffic, you will almost certainly lose money. You are paying for education and research when you begin and get your first few thousand clicks. If you are expecting to turn on paid traffic and collect sales or leads in twenty-four hours without having worked out your funnel, you won't – but sometimes leads come in on day one, which is fun.

But learning to use paid traffic is one of the safest and most reliable investments your business can employ. Because once you've figured out profitable paid channels, you can turn them on and off at will, depending on how full your sales pipeline is.

The main number you need to figure out for making sense of paid traffic is the absolute maximum you can afford to pay per customer, and keep the acquisition cost lower.

Why is paid just so good? Social media takes effort and

engagement, PR takes newsworthy stories and pitches, SEO can sometimes drop out and leave you without traffic . . . but companies will always be willing to take your money in exchange for traffic. You can count on that.

Yes, sometimes advertisers get blocked from Facebook, or Google, or some other traffic provider, but there's always another traffic provider willing to step in while you resolve the problem.

Let's start growing this tree branch and learn the basics of paid history and work our way up to the freshest options for paid traffic.

## 8.1 Traditional, Programmatic and Native Advertising

When people get into buying ads there can be some confusion about the differences between the available forms of advertising. I've read many articles that make it sound like it's native advertising vs programmatic – it's not.

Online you either buy ads in a traditional or programmatic way. Native advertising can take traditional or programmatic form but specifies a specific kind of advertising.

So:

- **Traditional advertising**: You negotiate with an agency/media buyer who negotiates with an ad-sales person at a publication for ad inventory. Expensive.

- **Programmatic advertising**: You negotiate directly with the publication through software to buy ad inventory. Cheaper. Often no middleman is present and the process is automated, involving Real Time Bidding (RTB) to allow multiple bidders to compete for the best slots available – kinda like eBay. *Mad Men* to *Maths Men*. Key weakness: sometimes your ads won't show due to ad blockers.

- **Native advertising**: Like advertorials of old. Advertising that looks like editorial content. Getting the publication's editorial involved is ideal for matching tone (this makes it traditional). This can include product placement and sponsorships. Sometimes native ads can also be bought through software without much of a human element (making it mostly programmatic). But true native ads are matched specifically to an individual publication.

All right, let's get into all the main options you've got.

## 8.2   Google's Advertising Options (Programmatic)

### AdWords search

If you've done any online advertising this is probably where you started, creating text ads that appear on Google search for terms that carry buyer intent.

The challenge with this option is that the demand is at an all-time high so the supply cost of ad inventory keeps rising. The cost per click often falls between £1 and £2. Competitive clicks can easily break £10 a click (some legal clicks can cost over £100) and at that level competitors are trying to outplay each other, using business-intelligence software to reverse engineer each other's strategy.

But for many industries AdWords is very effective and an essential part of their sales and lead generation. Yet the costs will keep going up.

If you are getting into this space and have up to a couple of thousand a month to spend, read Perry Marshall's *Ultimate Guide to Google AdWords* (Entrepreneur Press, 2014). It's excellent. Just don't sign up for the book supplements if you want to protect your email inbox from an onslaught (!).

If you have more than a few thousand to spend each month, don't do it yourself, hire an agency that does this full time. They'll probably charge 10 to 15 per cent of your ad spend plus some base rate, but you'll make that money back fast on the improvement in results.

Luke Alley reminds me that Google is constantly innovating with new ad types, ad targeting and other innovations to help advertisers see better returns. These innovations mean more quality traffic for companies who use them right.


### AdWords display

The advantage with Google display is that these ads are usually cheaper than search ads – but it can be far less effective. If you are starting to play with display, try starting with these three popular sizes: 300×250, 728×90, 120×600.

I've had some great results by doing my research and telling Google a list of websites I want my ads to show up on. Google's DoubleClick Ad Exchange is your friend here.

Display often works best for upper-funnel searches: people who are not ready to purchase but are doing research. So offering demos, newsletter signups or whitepapers, etc, in exchange for some info works best. Just no-obligation stuff.

Try also comparing those results with mobile campaigns. The three sizes to start with here: 300×250, 300×50, 320×50.

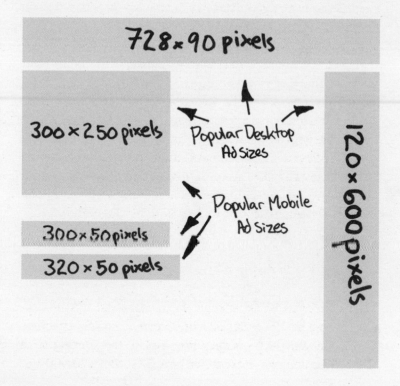

## YouTube and Facebook video

The YouTube advertising option is found in AdWords in the video section. Clicks from YouTube are quite cheap but they take much more work to set up because you have to have the right kind of video.

You can also target 'YouTube' as a placement in the Display Network and get those text ads that overlay YT videos. Luke's seen good results from this.

I quite like Tommie Power's video training in this space (tommiepowers.com), if you or one of your team wants to do it in-house. He's *very* casual in his presentations, and the production level isn't anything fancy, but his tactics work and he's funny.

If you are only going to do one thing with video at first, try building a remarketing list in AdWords and running your video on that list. People come to your website, they leave, and then they see you on YouTube in the next few weeks. Just don't overdo impressions-per-user or it gets creepy.

Facebook video advertising is harder to crack because people don't like getting marketed to here, but the targeting is fantastic and you can also run retargeting campaigns. Definitely go for entertainment over education on Facebook if you can swing that way.

## 8.3 Yahoo and Bing (Programmatic)

Depending on which country you live in, this might not be worth even looking at. Here in the UK Google has almost

90 per cent of the search market, with Yahoo and Bing taking about 10 per cent.

But in the USA, 33 per cent of the search market uses Bing and Yahoo. It's also worth noting that Bing and Yahoo are partners who share each other's ad inventory for the most part, so if you are using one, you are using both. Luke finds that Yahoo and Bing are similar in ad performance to AdWords.

## 8.4   Ad Networks (Native and Programmatic)

While providers like Google AdWords offer per-click pricing, behind the scenes they are selling ad inventory at CPM. CPM = Cost Per Mille, 'mille' being Latin for thousand. While it's safer for low-budget advertisers to pay by the click, once you start buying higher amounts of ad inventory, you'll want to pay by 1,000 impressions.

### What is real-time bidding (RTB)?

If you are involved in financial markets, perhaps something like eTrade with instantaneous auctions, you know what RTB is about. Advertisers all bid on impressions and if the bid is won the buyer's ad is displayed on the publisher's website in real time.

The publications might sell some of their ad space the traditional way, directly negotiating with the advertiser. The premium inventory can be sold this way. But they usually use a programmatic for the rest by selling their impressions to a supply-side platform.

- **Supply-side platform**: serves the publishers providing ad inventory

- **Demand-side platform**: serves the advertisers wanting to buy ad inventory

You can get at those ads by working with a demand-side platform (DSP) to undertake the RTB process.

One popular demand-side platform software is Site Scout. You can use them as long as you have at least £350 to begin. I will warn that I'm not the first person to blow £700 in something like an hour because I didn't set up the right throttle on ad-spend. Don't do what I did. It felt like I blinked and I was £700 lighter and had no results to show. But SiteScout lets you find a large list of relevant publishers and specifically target your ads there, using things like day parting (running ads only at the best hours of the day) to keep good ROI. Their remarketing is solid too.

## 8.5   Popular Native-Advertising Options

You've seen these everywhere but they may have flown under your nose. They are usually in the form of sponsored articles that you find at the bottom of other articles on larger online publications, that say 'you might also enjoy' or something similar.

You can only use blog post and articles that are not salesy on most of the native-advertising providers. The traffic is rather cheap, anywhere between 7 to 20 pence per person, but it provides a very high bounce rate and is usually mobile or tablet traffic. The traffic might bounce but it does spend time on the page. This is why I love using this funnel with native traffic:

*Native ad → article → retargeting →*
*follow-up article with lead magnet*

## Outbrain

The largest provider is Outbrain and on my first play with them I was getting traffic back to my website from *Rolling Stone* magazine, *Time* and *Fortune* at about 10 pence per person. Cool.

To have success with Outbrain it's good to allow a month to run your content, this allows their algorithm to find the publications that send the most traffic and prioritize your article promotion there. And make sure that you are only trying to promote articles. If you are sending people to a squeeze page or a sales page you'll have your campaign terminated. Real people check the campaign before it goes live.

## Taboola

Perhaps the second most popular native-ad provider. If you are trying to get traffic to a page with a dash of sales to it, perhaps an eBook in exchange for an email address, you can often get away with this on Taboola. Their traffic is a few pence cheaper than Outbrain's and not as strict. The downside is that the traffic is of lower quality, in my experience, and their analytics don't seem to be very accurate. Still a good option if Outbrain isn't a fit.

Native advertising really isn't that great without retargeting, in my opinion. It's not traffic that converts very well on your website on first visit. But because of the low cost and the high volume you can crank website-traffic volume and get a good volume of people on your retargeting list.

## Boosting PR results with native ads

So let's say you have hired a PR agency and they landed you a really good article on a publication that people trust. The problem is that only a couple of thousand people have seen it. Enter native advertising to the rescue.

If you act fast and boost the PR article with native-ad promotion you can quickly scale the reader count. Why would you want to do this? Well the cost of the PR efforts will probably be up there and you don't want to leave the fate of readership count to organic numbers. Pour gas all over that article and make it far more popular.

Depending on how far you want to push it, if you do it the same day that the article gets published you can often get the article in the 'most-read article' section on the publication's homepage, and even more organic views will go there. Combine native advertising with social-media paid promotion, and all at once you can turn a good PR placement into a massive attention-getter that carries more trust than if it appeared on your own website. And if you have a link in the PR article back to your website, watch the warm traffic flow.

It's worth mentioning that the link will probably be good for your website SEO, so for kicks and giggles why not build links back to this article along with the paid promotion. Value in so many ways.

Native advertising is just getting started. I think it's obvious that a higher advertising budget will shift from outbound-type ads to inbound ads and native will take a huge part of the total market budget.

## 8.6   Mobile First: Google vs Facebook vs Apple

It's worth pointing out the mobile battle that's begun between Google, Facebook and Apple. Ad blocking is getting nasty on mobile between the two giants, Google and Apple.

With iOS9, iPhones and tablets are taking a cheap shot at Google. Blocking ads is good for the mobile user as it saves data costs and makes the reading experience much easier. As a marketer I wish this wasn't so, because I know the quality of content will take a hit, there often being no other revenue stream for publications outside of advertising. Reduce that income stream and journalists and content creators who have a publication and can't afford proprietary ad-tech lose jobs. And the end user who loves ad-free reading inadvertently loses the content they enjoy because they don't support the revenue stream.

Facebook can still run ads on iPhones because it's in its own app. But look at what Apple and Facebook are trying to do with Apple News and Facebook is doing with Instant Articles: they are trying to push content from other publishers through their service, stripping out their ads, adding their own and distracting the public from what's going on by saying it's for speed's sake. Ugly.

If you are turning your website into a small publisher, get ready to lose traffic and any ads you might be running on your own site.

Have a read: filipmatous.com/apple-vs-google-vs-facebook (this will redirect you to the *Verge* article).

## 8.7   Retargeting

If there is just one form of advertising you are paying for, this is usually the one I recommend to start with. This is because it's often some of the best cheaper traffic that comes to your site. And it's all warm traffic.

Retargeting requires your audience to have already come to your site so that you can add them to your retargeting list. It works by placing a pixel on the page(s) whose viewers you want to add to a list.

To be factually correct I need to add that you can actually use retargeting by placing your pixels on any website that you own, and then market to the audience that comes to that page. You can even make a deal with other business websites that have products complementary to yours and place pixels on each other's websites for an easy way to trade relevant traffic. I've heard you can even add people to retargeting lists from emails, but I've not yet done that. It's on my list to test.

## 8.8   Perfect Audience and AdRoll: the big retargeting all-in-one providers

Perfect Audience and AdRoll work roughly in the same way, and having used both, Perfect Audience is my favourite. Both allow you to retarget to Facebook, Twitter, Google and other ad networks.

Of course you can go individually to Twitter or Facebook or Google to access detailed retargeting options but often the convenience of having everything in one place out-weighs the fine tuning you can do individually.

I will say though that it really makes sense to use the right tool for the job. On Twitter-heavy projects I'll use the retargeting option directly from Twitter, as they are better than anything either Perfect Audience or AdRoll can give me.

LinkedIn is also getting into the retargeting game, but at this point you need to spend a lot with them to gain access to this.

## 8.9 Legalities and Pages You'll Need on Your Website.

When you start pushing traffic make sure you are aware of what each platform requires you to disclose in the privacy and cookies pages on your website. Not doing this can get you banned and your advertiser account terminated. This happens to people all the time so don't risk it. It may take you fifteen minutes to update your website: do it and stay safe.

And one tip: **Avoid** pop-ups and screen-takeovers. These can jam with the rules that paid traffic requires and even though they are in vogue with many marketers, ask yourself: do you actually *like* pop-ups?

Empathize.

Most people hate pop-ups and yes, they often increase opt-in rates from first-time visitors, but at what cost? One test I was reading lately said that the percentage of people clicking the X to get rid of the pop-up was in the high 90s. I think that in the future marketers will shake their heads at us for abusing our website visitors with that nonsense and dragging our brand class down.

# 9:

## PR TRAFFIC

If you've worked with PR agencies in the past, this scenario may sound familiar:

Following the pitch from the PR agency, you agree with the thirty- or forty-something-year-old director who pitched that you want to begin.

The first few months are exciting; you start getting coverage and feel taken care of. But you notice that pretty much all your interactions are with early-twenty-somethings. No sign of the original director.

Then, month four through to month nine seems less impressive. You just don't feel romanced like you were at the start. You look to end the contract.

Not all, but many larger agencies expect this churn and have their directors worry about closing the next client while the twenty-somethings do all the work. They don't expect you to stick around long-term.

This is why I usually recommend smaller businesses, who hire solo PRs, or boutique agencies. They need your loyalty and will work for it far harder than the big guys with big accounts who the directors wine and dine, leaving the small/medium accounts to junior staff.

But with all this, I am a huge fan of PR's impact on traffic, when it's done right.

## 9.1: PR's Traffic Benefits

Here's a short list of what good PR can do specifically for your website traffic:

- **Social Proof**: Those brand mentions on trustworthy publications can be used as trust signals on your website. 'As seen on . . .' Visitors usually consider press coverage to be a sign of a healthy business and it is a proven website conversion-rate booster.

- **SEO Boost**: Links from online press coverage are the most valuable links you can get if you want to boost your rankings and volume of traffic coming from Google. In the last couple of years a symbiotic relationship between SEO agencies and PR agencies has formed that strengthens both professions.

- **Warm/Hot Traffic**: Just as in offline life, people won't believe you if you say nice things about yourself, others must do this. Online, having someone read an article that involves you takes the temperature of the traffic from cold to warm or even hot if it's an impressive piece. Then they hit Google to search your brand or follow the link to your website and the chances of them becoming a lead shoot up.

- **Content Marketing Upgrade**: Sure, you can use your social media, email and paid channels to distribute self-made content, but swap that content with a trustworthy PR piece and in many cases you'll get more brand impact and quality traffic at the Interest stage flowing to your website.

## Selling property: An example of PR-driven website conversions

One former property client used PR in a very strategic way to gain access to a network of high-net-worth property developers.

The client's goal was to get to know persons X, Y and Z, and enter the relationship as a peer.

To achieve this goal a couple of things were created: luxurious video of the state of property in the area, a micro-site with its own brand, and a physical event for the video screening.

This was the funnel:

*Teaser PR coverage → micro-site with video teaser → invite to physical event → desired relationships*

Second funnel, post-event:

*Event PR coverage → people view video on micro-site → client gets more branding as an expert*

It started with an educational industry video being commissioned by the client to shortlist a dozen people in the industry who the client wanted to know on a better level.

Filming of about fifteen people, including X, Y and Z, took place while a micro-site with a brand unconnected with the client was created.

Teaser of the video is uploaded to the micro-site. The fifteen people filmed for the video are listed with name and photo under the video. The client is somewhere in the middle, looking just like one of the people interviewed, not like the person funding the whole project. Press are reached out to and invited to the event; the first round of press goes live online, sending traffic back to the micro-site with video teaser, increasing interest.

Physical film screening occurs, everyone in the film shows up and press shows up to write about the state of the industry.

The client gets an evening of drinks with people he wanted to build a relationship with.

The press release an event summary and the video is released in full for the public to view. More branding for everyone involved. The client ends up doing work with some of the people he wanted a relationship with. Huge ROI on a marketing campaign that cost under 50K all in.

## 9.2   Indirect Traffic

It's very common to see your website's direct and organic traffic increase in the first one to three days after an article is published. Even if the article doesn't have a link, I've seen that some people who are interested in the story will often Google you or put in your homepage URL right after reading.

Look in your analytics if that is happening. Also it's a wise idea to monitor Twitter to see if anyone there is sharing your article. You can simply pop the article URL in Twitter's search bar, or better, use SproutSocial or Hootsuite to get alerts any time someone shares it. By monitoring who is sharing it, you can tweet them back or email them referencing the article, if they match the type of person you are trying to reach.

## 9.3: Understanding Journalists' Needs

Susannah Breslin, a journalist and contributor for *Forbes*, had this to say about how she makes money at *Forbes*:

> I am paid a flat fee every month. Let's call this X. If I reach a certain traffic goal, I get paid an additional sum. Let's call that Y. Right now, X and Y are the same amount. So I double my money if I reach my traffic goal. The traffic goal is based on the number of unique visitors who visit my blog every month. If I exceed my traffic goal, I am paid a certain amount for every unique visitor I get over my monthly traffic goal. Let's call that Z. Your paycheque = X + Y + Z.*

Now this doesn't happen at every publication but it illustrates a point. Publications usually make their money through advertising. Sometimes subscriptions are also a part of their business model. The more eyeballs they have on their content, the more they can charge for their ad inventory.

Add to this that many journalists are churning out five articles a day and are underpaid. If you are trying to get a story published it should positively answer these considerations *for the journalist*:

- **Content match**: Will this story match what my readers want to learn or be entertained by?

---

* http://www.forbes.com/sites/susannahbreslin/2011/04/06/how-to-become-a-forbes-blogger/

- **Reach**: Is this likely to bring a lot of page views?

- **Effort**: How much work do I have to put into this to turn it into a story?

- **Exclusivity**: Can I have this as an exclusive so that I'm not competing with other publications?

To oversimplify: make the journalist's job easy and you'll get rewarded with coverage and traffic.

# 10:

## EMAIL, DIRECT AND DARK-SOCIAL TRAFFIC

Dark Social, if you haven't heard the term, is going to make a lot of sense. It involves email traffic and a host of other sources. But first, let's learn to track email traffic as it comes back to your website.

We're going to talk about four separate email types:

1. Personal Emails

2. Newsletters

3. Campaigns

4. Autoresponders

## 10.1: Personal Emails

You are probably using an email signature. But are you tracking how many times people use it to go to your website? More than that, do you know which employee email generates the most website visits and what those visitors do?

Here's how you can track email signatures for yourself and your team in UTM. If you are doing this for a team, the campaign section will use each person's name. The medium and source stays the same (for a shortcut to a UTM URL-builder, see: filipmatous.com/utm):

- Medium: email

- Source: signature

- Campaign: name

Just hyperlink your email signature with this custom URL instead of the naked website URL and you are set.

Avoid using URL shorteners in email as these can signal spam. But if you are in a sales function you might want to use Hubspot's email add-on called Sidekick. You'll learn not only if your email was opened or clicked, but when, how many times, from which location, and on what kind of device.

Yeah, it's a bit creepy how much we can Big-Brother from an email. In all practicality this is usually overkill, but for that important email or pitch, this tool comes in handy.

If you don't use any kind of tracking your traffic will almost always be lumped in with direct traffic in your analytics.

## 10.2 Newsletters

The two metrics you need to know when it comes to email:

- **Open rate**: The percentage of people on your newsletter list that open your email

- **Click-through rate**: The percentage of people that click through to your website

How these two are affected starts with the quality of the list, because a crappy email list won't do much even if you send an incredible emailing. But if your list is quality, it can drive some HOT traffic.

An email list of 1,000 true subscribers who want to hear from you can outperform a list of a million sloppily collected emails.

Got a good-to-great email list? Here are the main variables that affect your ultimate outcome, in which your subscribers, clicking through the email to your website, convert to whatever goal you have set up.

Email variables:

- Time of the day
- Day of the week
- Topic quality
- Subject
- Pre header
- Sender's name
- CTA button/link format

How they affect open-rate and click-through rate:

| Email Variables | Open % | Click % | Notes |
|---|---|---|---|
| Time of the day | | | Depends on persona (and day of the week) |
| Day of the week | | | Depends on persona (and time of the day) |
| Content quality | | | Most important variable + persona match |
| Subject title | | | Subject interdependent with topic quality |
| Pre header | | | Helpful if it supports the subject |
| Sender's name | | | Level of trust is crucial + consistency |
| Email format | | | This includes copy, photos, html & font |
| CTA format | | | Test plain links vs buttons, and placement |

| Impact Level | Key | How To Improve |
|---|---|---|
| Crucial | | |
| High | | Once you get all the major best practice out of the way, the best way to improve is volume of emails sent and A/B testing ONE variable at a time. Do two variables at a time and you muddy the learnings |
| Medium | | |
| Medium/Low | | |
| Low | | |
| Very Low | | |
| None | | |

Try these tips to increase the volume of traffic back to your website from your newsletters:

- **Sender's name**: Keep this consistent with each newsletter mailing

- **Subject**: Keep this under sixty characters whenever possible, to look good on mobile, otherwise you'll get the dreaded '. . .'

- **Pre header**: Keep this under fifty characters whenever possible. The pre header is the very top of the email in small copy and rarely read by anyone once the email is opened. Just there to increase open rate.

- **Body copy**: The number-one question to keep in mind when writing this part is 'Why the heck would someone want to give me their time and click the link to my website?'

## 10.3 Email Campaigns

This section deals with doing a one-off email to announce something on your website, or when a partnering company is doing an email announcement for you and trying to send interested visitors to your website.

Example: We were marketing an event for a client and had help from two brands on the email-marketing front.

One was a well-known brand that was an event partner. The other brand was a trade magazine that matched our personas. We exchanged £1,800 for this mailing.

Here's how they did (note ticket sales, as this is the main metric):

### Brand 1: Event partner with a 7,679-strong email list

25 per cent open rate = 1,890 people opened it

7.3 per cent click-through rate (from unique opens) = 560 people clicked

5 per cent conversion rate (from unique clicks) = 28 tickets sold

### Brand 2: Trade magazine with a 16,000-strong email list

?? per cent open rate (wouldn't disclose)

Click-through rate = 19 people clicked

5 per cent conversion rate = 1 ticket sold

Brand 1 was more than twenty-five times more valuable for us than brand 2, and the corresponding email over fifty times more effective. That sounds crazy but it is common: brands that take care of their list have hot traffic, brands that neglect their list have dead-weight names who don't open the emails or click.

A common problem is abusing the list with countless asks. If you are paying some brand for an email shot, ask to see their typical open and click-through rates. You don't want to be paying for a list that is hammered every day with different offers. Lists die when this happens.

## 10.4 Email Automation (aka Autoresponders)

You want hot traffic to come back to your website for conversions. An incredibly popular and proven method is through email automation.

Email automation is a series of emails that you set up that so once someone opts in for, say, a whitepaper on your website they automatically start getting emails from you.

The trick to ensuring that these work is to ensure that they *do not suck*.

'Do not suck'?!

Most email sequences out there suck because they 'sell, sell, sell' and fail to empathize with the reader, giving them value to the point where they feel like the read was worth their time and they want more. You need the email to match the reader's needs and for it to be delivered at the right time.

If all you do is promote your stuff and tell people to click this and that, watch your opt-out rate rise (people unsubscribing). Also watch your abuse reports: if those creep above 1 in 1,000 you are doing something wrong and may get your domain blacklisted (designated as spam) from the major email providers.

Probably the best read on this is Andre Chaperon's *Autoresponder Madness*. His strategy on building narrative and increasing earnings per subscriber (EPS) contains important lessons in getting people to click to your website with intent.

The email sequence usually runs anywhere from three emails all the way to fifteen. But typically you only need five. There might be breakout sequences too, where you ask people to click something, they do (showing interest), and your automation moves them from the original email series onto a new series that keeps in mind what they expressed interest in.

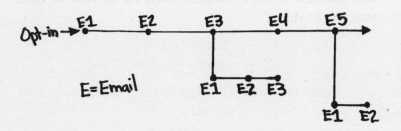

If you are after hot traffic – and of course you are – then this is pretty much unavoidable. You'll need to know the basics.

## 10.5 Dark Social

I was sitting around a table a couple of months ago with stakeholders of a key business publication and the topic of dark social came up. They estimated that close to 70 per cent of their direct traffic was social traffic.

I've found in many cases that while you can track social traffic coming from Twitter, Facebook, LinkedIn and other public networks – a huge amount of social traffic is mislabelled as direct traffic. Dark social.

### Culprits of direct traffic that aren't actually direct

These are just traffic sources without any referral information attached to them, which shows up in your website analytics as 'direct':

- **Chat**: WhatsApp, Skype, Messenger, Slack, etc, none of them pass any referral information.

- **Email**: Almost none of the email providers out there will pass any referral information.

- **Apps**: Any time you click a link in an app it will open a browser in the app or open a new window. The browser goes directly to the site so it shows up as direct.

- **Https**: If traffic is coming from a secure site, the referral won't pass (this is an increasing problem as more sites are going secure).

- **Organic search**: Some of the referral traffic from Google is set up in certain browser configurations to show up as direct.

The first one, chat, is all social (pure dark social, if I may). Email can be social too. And Apps are a mixed bag but usually also from a social function.

How does dark social actually play out? Using examples from my life, this is how I have contributed to dark social in just the last twenty-four hours:

- My fiancée texted me a link to a vintage furniture shop she wants to visit
- I sent a link to a blog post on analytics to a group on WhatsApp
- My designer sent me an article on sexy wireframes over Slack
- A friend sent me a link over email to his updated video portfolio
- I messaged a mate over Facebook with a link to a band website

In a given week, think how many times you receive and send links to websites without doing it publicly. Compare it to how often you do it publicly. Both are social, yet only one shows up as such in your website analytics.

So what should you do?

Take an honest look at your website.

### Sharing

- Do you make it easy for people to email each other a link?
- Is your mobile version of the site a candidate for a share with a WhatsApp button?

### Tracking

In every case that you can, are you tagging your URLs with UTM so it shows up properly in your analytics, so you can make better-informed decisions about future marketing efforts?

Yes many/most people will just copy and paste your URL, but you can at least add another 40 per cent of that traffic into the right buckets instead of it ending up in direct.

Let's roll into the last – short but important – part of this book. Tracking, measuring, reporting and goal setting.

Helloooo Successville.

# Part Three

# MEASUREMENT AND OPTIMIZATION

We've been avoiding figures for the sake of learning the main concepts, but let's dive into the numbers. Thankfully these three chapters are short as they are rather dry. But if you can take action on what you are about to read, it will give you a strong mental framework for making smart decisions that increase how much your website is noticed.

You will learn:

- How to pick the right metrics to track for your business and understand analytics (moving past visitors counts)

- How to cut the fat and optimize how you get your website noticed

- How to set web-traffic goals and create a two-page report that keeps you on track month over month

# 11:

## ANALYTICS AND METRICS

Quick primer:

- **Metrics**: Standard measure. Data that's useful for answering questions that need information. Tangible and focused on the past. Example: *We had 600 people sign up to our newsletter this month, an improvement of 250 over last month.*

- **Analytics**: Logical analysis. Useful for answering questions that relate to strategy and insight. Intangible and focused on the future. Example: *What did we do that caused this significant improvement in opt-ins and how can we keep this momentum or increase it?*

Often these two work together in the following way for website traffic:

*Metrics → Analytics → Insights → Better Decisions →*
*More quality traffic*

If you don't have metrics, it's hard to do logical analysis – this informs the insights you need to make better decisions – which bring you more website traffic – which impacts your ultimate goal: growing your business.

Most of you will access these metrics in Google Analytics, but the terms and metrics are consistent across all the major analytics platforms.

Here are some of the popular metrics and questions that kick off good analytical thinking.

## 11.1  In What Ways Are People Reading Our Articles?

This technical question was asked a couple of months ago when I was analysing an investigative-journalism website. Main goal: get more traffic and improve the website reading experience.

*Relevant metrics*

- **Users**: Number of unique devices that went to the site.

- **Bounce rate**: Percentage of users that just viewed one page and then left the site.

- **Devices**: How many users came individually via mobile, tablet and desktop.

- **Time on page**: Take special care to only measure time on page from traffic that doesn't bounce – more on this later.

What the monthly metrics showed us (I rounded the numbers to illustrate):

- **Mobile**: 60,000 visits, 99 per cent bounce rate, average time on page: 1.5 minutes.

- **Tablet**: 20,000 visits, 90 per cent bounce rate, average time on page: 3.5 minutes.

- **Desktop**: 50,000 visits, 80 per cent bounce rate, average time on page: 3 minutes.

Then we compared the traffic from the same month a year earlier, and specifically looked at device usage: desktop traffic had dropped by 10 per cent, mobile increased by 5 per cent and tablet increased by 15 per cent.

### Analysis and insights

Mobile really isn't showing good engagement yet. Tablet users are spending time reading but not showing much interest in more than one article: seems to be rapidly growing in popularity. Desktop is doing fine, engagement-wise, but dropping in popularity.

We also looked at these metrics that weren't as crucial:

- Traffic by days of the week

- Popular hours of the day

- Social engagement with articles

### Decisions from all the insights

In this case, mobile design should be the priority of focus for the new website design as the majority of traffic comes from phones. When something is a priority it usually means the budget gets shifted to that place.

## 11.2 A Short List of Important Metrics

Let's explore the main metrics you should be aware of, and then I'll provide some further reading for those who want to get a foundational education in analytics.

### Important paid-traffic metrics

*Attention level*

How to measure the traffic before it gets to your website:

- **CPC: Cost Per Click** – smaller campaign budgets usually use this.

- **CPM: Cost Per Mille** – the cost of 1,000 impressions. Larger campaign budgets usually use this metric to measure traffic.

- **CTR: Click-Through Rate** – ratio of people that click a link to total number of people presented with the option.

### Important website metrics

*Interest, desire, and action level*

How to measure what the traffic does once it's on your website. Utterly incomplete, but something to get you thinking about how these metrics could apply to your business:

- **CTR: Click-Through Rate:** Ratio of people that

click a link to total number of people presented with the option.

- **Users**: You can use sessions and visitors, but users is the lowest number because it combines all the sessions by specific device, which is the closest you can get to the actual amount of humans on your website.

- **New visitors**: Important for measuring interest.

- **Repeat visitors**: Important for measuring desire. In most cases, repeat visits are far warmer and more valuable than new users.

- **Top content**: Have a look at your top ten. What are my most popular pages? Which ones are ignored? Why?

- **Bounce rate**: Ratio of people who only visit one page on your website and then leave, no matter how long they spend on that page. Which pages do people come to and exit? Blogs and articles will have very high bounce rates and that's normal.

- **Exit**: Which pages do people leave the site from? Contact pages, for example, should have a high exit ratio.

- **Conversion rate**: What's the ratio of people on a page that take the specific action you want them to?

- **CPA: Cost Per Action**: How much does it cost for people to take action. Also answers 'How much am I spending to get that sale or lead?' Profitable traffic is when the CPA is lower than the profit margin. Also known as the customer-acquisition cost.

- **AOV: Average Order Value**: How much do people order on average? Split this apart by traffic channel to see if some channels have different averages.

- **LV: Lifetime Value**: How much do people spend on average during the whole lifecycle of being a customer? Impossible for startups but companies with history will know this.

## Important email metrics

If you are analysing how good your email campaigns are for driving traffic, you'll want to look at all of these:

- **Open rate**: Most email providers provide industry standards: is yours above the standard?

- **Click-through rate**: This metric shows up everywhere, eh? If people are opening your emails but not clicking your links, ask what you can do to change that.

- **Open count**: If someone shows as having opened an email over twenty times it's safe to assume they forwarded it to a team or network. Pay special attention to these people as they may be brand advocates and you should find excuses to talk to them.

- **Conversion rate**: Once the email traffic hits your website, what ratio takes your desired action?

- **Opt-in rate**: Ratio of people who choose to subscribe.

- **Opt-out rate**: Ratio of people who unsubscribe when you do a mailing. Is it above or below the industry standard? Why?

## Important social metrics

These metrics are found on pretty much every social network, they might just use different names:

- **Like**: Often the least valuable for gaining traffic.

- **Share**: Often the most valuable for gaining traffic.

- **Comment**: Most important for engagement which can then impact traffic.

- **Follow**: Most valuable for long-term warm traffic.

## Further reading

*Keeping Up with the Quants: Your Guide to Understanding and Using Analytics*, by Thomas Davenport and Jinho Kim: great for non-analysts seeking to understand how to talk about analytics and what questions to ask their analysts.

*Digital Metrics Field Guide*, by Stephen D. Rappaport: a comprehensive list of almost every digital-marketing metric that exists; will make you think about logical questions you didn't even consider might matter.

# 12:

## PEOPLE AND EGOS

The number-one hardest part of my career isn't making the strategy work – that chess game keeps getting better. No, *the most challenging part is also the best part*: meeting and working with all kinds of people who test me.

You might be used to breaking hard news to employees, a partner, a boss or a supplier. But if you are new to taking a scientific approach to websites that involves measuring and managing traffic, then managing people who don't fit is going to end up being the hardest part of what you do.

All the moving parts of traffic and websites are made by people, for people. And since you have to measure things to improve, you are usually the first person who discovers the weak links. Transparency is great for improvement but also requires you to let go of those who are not moving the project forward.

If you watch *The Profit* (currently it's my favourite American TV show), you'll hear the star, Marcus Lemonis, repeat the same thing in every episode when he's fixing and scaling a broken business. That business is made up of three things:

- People
- Process
- Product

A business needs at least two of the three to be good, in

order to survive. The businesses that scale have all three. You'll become the process person when it comes to the online part of the business if you do what's in this book. You'll rip up or optimize and restructure the process depending on what state it is in.

Best-case when working with teams: you'll find the right people in the right places. Or it's a bit more difficult because you have the right people in the wrong places. Worst-case: you have the wrong people and you need to let them go.

Once you set the website goals that we will discuss in the final chapter, what you need to do becomes obvious.

If you are like me, you'll end up investing in developing your emotional intelligence and mental toughness. This means you can stay emotionally healthy and go home in the evening with a clear mind.

## Pattern recognition

The more you look at analytics the more you'll start to see patterns that identify what is correlation and what is the actual causation. You might have someone in charge of Facebook, someone else in charge of AdWords, another agency doing your SEO.

Instead of increasing your overall online marketing spend and seeing an increase in conversions, you'll break apart the aggregate data and see the traffic sources individually, allowing you to fine-tune the overall performance.

Month over month you'll be looking at what you are spending on each traffic source by combing the traffic cost plus the labour cost and comparing it with the other traffic sources. It's too fast to make judgements in a month, but after three to five months (SEO will take longer) you should get a pretty good idea if a channel is going to achieve the goals your website has laid out. There is a testing period that can take a few months to dial down, but after that, if the channel isn't working, stop it and reallocate it to the next channel.

Where it gets tricky is deciding if the traffic channel doesn't work because:

- it's the wrong traffic channel

- the budget is wrong

- the wrong person is in place

If you don't have the skill set to know which one it is, this is where it makes sense to have a consultant look over your shoulder. If you are doing this small-scale, or on your own, you can find someone to look over the metrics by paying by the minute on Clarity.fm.

When you find a profitable channel, celebrate – and see how much scope there is to scale the volume. But never stop with one channel – that keeps you vulnerable. Having a few channels that are working for you, even if one channel is stronger than the others, is how you protect yourself against terminal risk. Diversify your channels so if one channel suddenly gets knocked down you can shift budget to the other channels, even if it is only temporary while you fix what is broken.

You might be lucky and never have a traffic source break on you, but it happens often enough, it's not a risk that you need. If your business has a single point of failure you'll know the stress. This single point of failure not only applies to the traffic sources, but to the people in charge of the traffic sources as well.

## Bit.ly example

I was auditing the social ROI for a boutique communications agency and saw they were doing Twitter communications for half a dozen clients. On glance I could tell that they were pushing little to no traffic back to their clients' websites. This information would not make a happy boss, so my first job was to add bit.ly to all the tweets moving forward.

After a month the data was conclusive. Most tweets received zero clicks and the ones that did rarely got more than ten clicks.

Aha.

Terrible ROI. So what's wrong?

Turns out that a new process and small promotional budget fixed everything. The new process for Twitter cut down the investment of labour by more than half and decreased all the tweet volume, refocusing on the type of tweets that made impact. A small promotional budget was put behind the tweets every week.

Twitter traffic grew to hundreds of clicks per tweet back to their client websites.

## Egos

We've all got them in various measures. I don't think that egos affect web traffic in a negative fashion – as long as they are kept in check by using transparency and accountability to agreed minimum KPIs.

But transparency requires your company culture to be totally okay with failure, as long as lessons are learned. I've worked with teams where it's expected to not get everything right and to learn from efforts that don't go well.

These teams, if they have the right people, end up with very successful online-traffic funnels. It's just a question of time. Because traffic growth and website conversions benefit from the scientific method you learned as a teenager in science class:

- Research

- Hypothesis

- Prediction

- Experimentation

- Conclusion

The leader needs to make people feel safe in order to show when the experiment's conclusion doesn't agree with the hypothesis. Hypothesis failure cannot threaten their job. As long as they did their research and you were there to agree to their hypothesis, the team should feel that it is okay to admit something didn't work as predicted.

If you are engaged with this process then you will make incorrect hypotheses too. It's important to highlight when you do get it wrong, in order to set an example.

But if you do commit to this transparent path, you'll have to take action if you realize you have the wrong person. It undermines the integrity of the rest of the team if you keep someone who just doesn't fit.

# 13:

## GOALS AND MONTHLY REPORTS

We've learned about all the moving parts involved in how to get your website noticed. In this last chapter let's bring them together and make it manageable.

One thing I advise is keeping it simple. Select the *one* website macro metric that makes the biggest impact and then find the supporting metrics. You want this key metric to be something you can refer to month over month, even year over year, to gauge overall progress.

Don't make that metric overall traffic, this is usually very unhelpful and removed from the story that's affecting conversions.

Whatever you choose is going to be the main metric that you try to improve, and the metric you discuss and compare every month.

The *supporting* metric(s) can either be macro or micro metrics:

- **Macro**:
  a metric that directly impacts a business goal

- **Micro**:
  assist metrics that help macro metrics occur

Some key metric examples (I recommend measuring these by month – or week/day, if you are in campaign mode):

### Sales-funnel metrics

- Average customer acquisition cost
- Average order value
- Amount of new customers
- Amount of repeat customers

### Lead-generation metrics

- Email inquiries via Contact page
- Conversion rate
- Phone-call inquiries from website's phone number (you can track this)
- Website visits from targeted company prospect list (works in B2B)

### Brand-marketing metrics

- New backlinks from publications and PR efforts
- Newsletter or autoresponder subscribers
- Brand-specific Google search visits

There are plenty more, but this is somewhere to start. And then there are the goals that assist the macro metrics, the *micro* metrics:

### Sales-funnel micro metrics:

- Tripwire product bought
- Webinar signed up to
- Brochure requested

### Lead-generation micro metrics

- Case-study downloaded
- Times that a site video was watched
- Lead-magnet requested (could be macro depending on what they give in exchange)

### Brand-marketing micro metrics:

- Time on site > 3 minutes
- Referral traffic from content marketing

## An example of how this might actually play out in a meeting

So once you've picked your main metric, think through how this might inform you when you plug it into the mental workflow we learned about earlier. We'll use newsletter subscribers as an example:

*Metrics → Analytics → Insights → Decisions → Improve Goal Conversions*

During the monthly meeting, the main metric review comes up. Monthly newsletter subscribers are around 500, when the monthly average is usually around 300. You want to know why the change occurred.

In analytics you pull apart all the sources providing traffic and you notice there are three that make up all of the sources:

- 270 subscribers from Facebook (150 more than average)

- 130 subscribers from Twitter (50 more than average)

- 100 subscribers from organic search traffic

You look at your top sources of content (metrics) and find that the spike came from one article. This article struck a nerve on Facebook and was shared repeatedly; some of that attention crossed over to Twitter as well.

Insight: Topic X seems to be doing well on Facebook.

Decision: Should we try another article in a similar vein to see if we can recreate the impact? Maybe we give the existing article a push with some paid budget on Facebook (it is being shared organically, after all)?

There really is no way to get around this. Just like in business, you must be intimate with the metrics in both traffic and website conversions, and know what those mean – in paid and labour costs – in order to make better decisions.

Don't get lost in the excitement of some traffic spike. Look for the unsexy metrics that are consistent month over month. If you've picked a metric that impacts your business, the insights will be easy to grasp and act on.

## Insights in two-page reports

Most people don't want massive reports when making decisions. If you work in a larger team and are in charge of reporting website and traffic results, try to fit everything you have in two pages. If you are good you shouldn't need loads of pages to review, as it takes skill and experience to pull out the insights people need to make decisions. Knowing which information to remove because it wastes time isn't easy.

I've produced a few too many fifty-page reports in the past and in most cases they didn't provide any more value than an insightful two-page report. In hindsight, these long reports probably harmed decision-making, demanding too much unnecessary cognitive effort. If you stick with the *metric + supporting metrics* concept you should be fine.

The main thing is to avoid making canned reports; the value is in the interpretation of the metrics to the point where you are suggesting a small number of options, or recommending one particular action.

# Conclusion

Well, you've done it. How is your knowledge tree looking now? I hope the trunk is in place so you can search out the smaller branches which are relevant to your website and business.

If you've enjoyed learning, visit filipmatous.com – say hi and join my newsletter. I write one informal email a month covering decisions business owners should be thinking about when it comes to websites and traffic (even unpacking things I try that fail).

It's a summary of the most important daily notes I jot down over the month to keep mentally sharp. Curating my notes into a newsletter saves time for non-marketing nerds who don't have time to trawl through the endless supply of quality and crap online.

Before I go, some one-sentence reminders to refresh what each of the thirteen chapters taught:

### Part One – How Your Website Strategy Impacts Your Business Goals

- Chapter 1. Websites and Pages: what we learned about A–I–D–A and how different types of traffic are required at the different stages, plus the various web pages you'll need.

- Chapter 2. Brand: how to think about web branding and finding your primary persona.

- Chapter 3. Traffic Funnels and Strategy: cold, warm and hot traffic – how to strategize the right funnel for your website and temperature.

- Chapter 4. Creating Content: matching content to where your persona is mentally.

### Part Two – Getting Noticed: Your Traffic Choices

- Chapter 5. Finding Traffic Sources: how to find the right traffic channels by uncovering your competitors' and industry favourites.

- Chapter 6. Organic Search Traffic: how to pick what terms to rank for, what to optimize on your website (30 per cent of the effort) and how to build links off site (70 per cent).

- Chapter 7. Social Traffic: how to pick the right networks – or none at all.

- Chapter 8. Paid Traffic: all the main choices available if you want to buy traffic (you should!).

- Chapter 9. PR Traffic: why it's a hard to get but awesome source of traffic.

- Chapter 10. Email, Direct and Dark-Social Traffic: the workhorses that send warm and hot traffic.

### Part Three – Measurement and Optimization

- Chapter 11. Analytics and Metrics: what to look for and what the numbers mean.

- Chapter 12. People and Egos: a candid look at people, process and product.

- Chapter 13. Goals and Monthly Reports: the foundation of increasing how many people notice your website.

One final thought on getting your website noticed. Add it alongside the tree trunk, right beside AIDA and empathy. When you are going through strategy and deciding on traffic sources, commit this to memory:

**– Quality traffic isn't cheap. It's profitable. –**

## Acknowledgements

Big thanks to the How To Academy and Pan Macmillan for giving me an excuse to take a month off work to reflect on the lessons I've learned after a decade in web traffic. I wonder what AIDA will look like in another decade.

**Big thanks to you, the reader,** for devoting the time to learn from my lessons and mistakes. I hope I shaved some serious time off your learning curve.

Finally big thank-yous to my mum and dad for feeding me while I worked silly hours to put this together. Talia for rushing into the study with Mr Meowsalot to distract me while I edited this. Sam for the years of laughs and friendship through many of these lessons. Paul for kicking my butt to go bigger. And finally Marius for making me feel normal about our never-satisfied approach to our respective crafts.

# Index